Praise

Very few leaders inherit a more difficult day-one situation in leadership than Jon Chasteen. I know because I was a part of the process of setting him in as the Lead Pastor of Victory Church in Oklahoma City. I have also been a fellow elder with Jon at Victory and a close friend since he took over. What I have witnessed over the past nine years is the transformation of a church and the emergence of a truly great leader. I highly recommend this book to everyone who needs encouragement and direction as you face your own challenges as a ReLeader.

Jimmy Evans
Bestselling Author
Founder of XO Marriage and Tipping Point

In the next decade, tens of thousands of pastors will get the call to take over the senior pastor role from an older pastor who's been in place for years or decades. It will rarely be easy. This is the powerful resource you're looking for to guide you through your assignment.

Carey Nieuwhof
Bestselling Author of *At Your Best*
Podcaster and Founder of The Art of Leadership Academy

Compelling. Inspiring. Motivating. Convicting. Redeeming. Clarifying. Affirming. *ReLeader* humorously and poignantly leads you on a journey to meet Jon Chasteen at his most vulnerable level. Not only will you want to read this book cover to cover, but you will also want to share it with every ReLeader you know.

Sam Chand
Author of *Leadership Pain*

This book is so needed right now in the body of Christ. We're living in a broken age, and we need to be taught how to rebuild the ancient ruins. Pastor Jon has lived this book. He has persevered and endured, emerging as a trusted voice for all of us.

Brady Boyd
Pastor of New Life Church

This may be the most important book for the Church in America today. We desperately need the next generation of Kingdom leaders to be prepared and equipped. There is a massive vacuum coming to the pulpits of our nation, and we don't have enough ReLeaders prepared to step in and take over. Thank you, Jon, for writing this book, for starting the *ReLeader* Podcast, and for sharing your anointed gift and experience.

Scott Wilson
Author of *Identity: The Search that Leads to Significance and True Success*
Founder and CEO of Ready Set Grow

Jon is the real-deal and has "ReLed" through difficult circumstances with a pure heart. Seamlessly blending biblical wisdom with real-world experiences, Jon offers a narrative that empowers leaders to revitalize culture and lead with faith. He is the perfect guide on this journey of "fixing stuff we didn't break." Read this book and learn from one of the best.

Dr. Rhonda Davis
Head of School of Bethesda Christian School

Jon has an excellent perspective on what it takes to be handed the reigns of an organization in the mist of leadership turmoil. It is a unique and difficult situation requiring great discernment, tenacity, patience, and emotional intelligence–all characteristics that Jon displays beautifully. I highly recommend this book!

Jimmy Witcher
Senior Pastor of Trinity Fellowship Church
Amarillo, Texas

My friend Dr. Jon Chasteen has a tremendous passion for connecting and supporting pastors and ReLeaders on their journey to bring healing to broken places. If you're in the special role of bringing revitalization, refreshing, and renewal, then this book is 100 percent for you.

Dino Rizzo
Executive Director of ARC

Without a doubt, Jon is one of the best leaders I know! In a world where many want to do their own thing, have an original vision, and make a name for themselves, Jon has found the beauty of rebuilding God-dreams that have fallen into ruin. Not everyone is called to be an Abraham. We need a whole lot more Isaacs who are simply willing to heal what is broken and build upon foundations that have already been laid. As we see so many churches stumbling and struggling to catch traction, Jon helps us all realize the practical things we can quickly enact to right the ship and start heading in the correct direction.

Aaron Kennedy
Pastor of Opendoor Church

Having witnessed Jon's incredible leadership journey and seen him walk with unwavering integrity through the toughest situations, I can attest that this book is a true testament to his resilience, wisdom, and ability to lead through the toughest challenges. *ReLeader* demonstrates how to navigate complex situations, inspire change, and leave a lasting impact. This book is a must-read for anyone seeking to lead effectively in any arena.

Wade Smith
Victory Church Leadership Team

Within the pages of this book, you'll discover the precious gift of grit. I've stood with Jon in the trenches of pastoring, parenting, and leading organizations, and his steadfast authenticity has consistently stood out in the face of adversity. Jon's insights and experience provide a roadmap for leaders in search of a trusted companion through the dares of ReLeading. To anyone brave enough to reinvent the status quo, this book is for you.

Oscar Ortiz
Victory Church Leadership Team

I've witnessed firsthand that these strategies are successful. When you face issues that could tempt you to put out the flame of your leadership, *ReLeader* encourages you to put another log on the fire.

Dale Swanson
Victory Church Leadership Team

Dr. Jon Chasteen

ReLeader

How To Fix What You Didn't Break

Dr. Jon Chasteen

ReLeader

How To Fix What You Didn't Break

ReLeader: How to Fix What You Didn't Break

ISBN: 978-1-960870-10-0 Paperback
ISBN: 978-1-960870-11-7 eBook

XLeadership is dedicated to empowering leaders with the knowledge, skills, and inspiration they need to excel in their respective fields. Our mission is to cultivate a new generation of leaders who not only navigate the challenges of their roles but also inspire positive change and foster growth within their organizations.

XLeadership, an imprint of XO Publishing
1021 Grace Lane
Southlake, TX 76092

Printed in the United States of America
24 25 26 27—5 4 3 2 1

Contents

Best Job I Ever Had

To the past and present staff of Victory Church. I cut my teeth in ReLeadership with you by my side. You are an amazing family of people who trusted, tolerated, and tempered me through some of the most difficult leadership years of my life. In doing so, you formed me into the leader I am today. Thank you for believing in me when I wasn't even sure I believed in myself. Thank you for being friends who stuck closer than a brother. Serving alongside each of you is one of the greatest joys of my life.

Foreword

Every leader leads.

Not every leader ReLeads.

ReLeading is for the courageous lunatic fringe who possess undeterrable faith in God and a tenacious boldness about His mission.

Why?

Because ReLeading comes with unique challenges and demands a different kind of leadership. Rather than building from the ground up, ReLeaders find themselves picking up the pieces of others' work and are typically forced to repair what someone else has broken. ReLeaders also often have to rebuild the trust of people who may have had their trust in a former leader violated.

If you're ReLeading, you probably find yourself running an obstacle course of problems, headaches, and conundrums as you seek to revitalize, restore, and reimagine the organization, team, or department you are leading. What you need is wise coaching from someone who's been there and done that.

I can't think of anyone better than one of my closest friends, Dr. Jon Chasteen. In this book, Jon will take you on a transformative journey into the world of ReLeading, providing unique and amazingly practical principles that have the power to revolutionize the way we approach leadership.

Jon is actually the person who first introduced me to the idea of ReLeading. We were working out, and between sets, Jon was sharing with me his experiences of accepting the lead pastor role of a church in the aftermath of the former pastor's moral failure. Jon patiently pastored hurting people, picked up the pieces, and worked to rebuild a broken culture. After navigating some tumultuous waters, the church is now stronger than it was before the crisis.

Jon then described taking the reins as president of a university that had seen more than its fair share of difficulties. During a break between sets of curls, Jon said something as if he'd realized it for the first time. The statement was simple yet profound. Jon said ...

"I fix broke stuff."

Technically, we both knew it would have been grammatically correct to say "broken" stuff. But two sweaty pastors from Oklahoma in the middle of a workout don't concern themselves with grammar.

Jon sat silent for a moment, and then he said thoughtfully, "I guess you could say I'm a ReLeader."

It was an epiphany. If we were cartoon characters, a lightbulb would have appeared over both our heads. It was as if Jon's words crystallized a leadership mantle countless leaders unknowingly accept and a leadership style those people need to master.

In that moment, I told Jon, "This is your next book." He tried to brush it off, but I could tell he realized he had just put into words something many leaders are living in but don't know how to describe.

This book may have been conceived in that conversation, but it's the result of Jon's wealth of experience, all the research he's done working with other leaders, and his deep study and understanding of God's Word.

Jon will invite you to reflect on your own leadership journey and the different ways you've stepped into the role of ReLeader. He'll give you a clear plan that you can customize to your particular situation. He'll help you see that within the challenges you're facing lie incredible opportunities for growth and transformation.

While the content of this book is stellar, what excites me even more about sharing it with you is the person who wrote it. Jon Chasteen is the embodiment of a ReLeader—someone who combines profound wisdom with practical, down-to-earth leadership insights. With a "Dr." in front his name and a heart full of humility, Jon's approach to leadership is refreshingly real. He doesn't offer lofty theories or abstract ideals; instead, he provides tangible, actionable advice that can be applied to your own leadership journey.

Jon's track record speaks for itself. Whatever he has ReLed, he has grown and made stronger.

As you embark on this journey, keep an open mind and a receptive heart. Jon's insights have the potential to reshape your approach to leadership, regardless of whether you lead a small team or a large organization. This book will help you lead with renewed focus and purpose.

Whatever it is you're leading, you can ReLead it into something better, and Jon is going to show you how.

Here's to your ReLeading success and impact!

Craig Groeschel
Pastor of Life.Church

Introduction

Some of you will rebuild the deserted ruins of your cities.
Then you will be known as a rebuilder of walls
and a restorer of homes

—Isaiah 58:12 (NLT)

I would call you a leader, but you're more than that. That title, "leader," is selling you short. It doesn't properly describe what you do. No offense to leaders, but you're something far greater.

- You didn't launch. You *re*launched.
- Your organization may be surviving, but it's not thriving.
- You're not building. You are *re*building.

That's what Isaiah called it. He said some of you are called to rebuild and will be known as *rebuilders.*

If that's you, then congratulations—you've received quite a calling. It's daunting and sometimes discouraging. But you already know that. I also hope you know that at the same time it is beautiful and close to the heart of God.

I didn't grasp any of that when I first started. In fact, it took me a while to even realize what God had created me to be: a *ReLeader.*

TO FIX BROKEN STUFF

A friend asked me if I would consider starting a roundtable group to train pastors in church planting and church growth.

Without hesitation, I replied, "I don't know how to plant churches. I've never done that. And quite frankly, I'm not really passionate about growing big churches. I'm more passionate about growing big people."

My friend is also a pastor. We knew each other quite well. So he looked at me kind of funny and asked, "Well, then, what is it that God has called you to do?"

What came out of my mouth next was like Mount Vesuvius.

It was as if I had an idea in me, words inside, that had been lying dormant. They were just waiting to come exploding out. In that moment they bubbled up to the surface and I blurted out, "I'm called to fix broken stuff."

That was it.

I had discovered my calling—my purpose.

I am a ReLeader.

Since you chose to read this book, the chances are that you are also a ReLeader. Perhaps you have just received language to describe something you've felt for a long time. In a leadership culture that spotlights launching, building, and growing, you may have struggled to name your calling and identify your tribe. You didn't launch your organization or start the department you now lead. You were placed there to follow someone else who occupied that position before you. Your office is in a building you did not build, you oversee a staff you did not hire, and you rely on systems you did not establish.

You, too, are a ReLeader.

Maybe you are just now recognizing that is what you are. The funny thing is that my conversation with my friend was the first time I had recognized the Mount Vesuvius within, although it had always been there. I had been a ReLeader for years.

LIFE IN THE RELEADER LANE

Yes, I drove a kidnapper's van, but I promise kidnapping was the furthest thing from my mind.

I had recently graduated college and taken a sales job that I didn't really want. Why did I do that? The reason was because I went to college to play basketball, but when I graduated, I was just as clueless about what I wanted to do with my life as when I had started. But I needed to do something, and I needed to make some money. My job sent me traveling all over Oklahoma, Arkansas, and Kansas to sell paper products to banks. So I was moving reams and pallets of paper and toner cartridges out of my nondescript, no windows, perfect-for-kidnapping company van. Frankly, it felt a lot like working at Dunder Mifflin for Michael Scott. For those of you unfamiliar with the sitcom *The Office,* the work the characters do is mind-numbingly boring, but it was a comedy, so humor was involved. Sadly, in my situation there was no comedy foil like Dwight Schrute to play practical jokes on. It was all paper products and no fun.

As it turns out, my region had been mismanaged and poorly led. In fact, it was the lowest performing sales territory in the company. That's not exactly the job anyone would dream about, and I was already feeling out of place. But in three short years I had built the accounts in that territory until it was one of the top performing regions in our entire company.

I didn't know it at the time, but God was already preparing the ReLeader in me.

While I was still selling paper to banks, I started a master's degree in education. After receiving the new degree, my undergraduate alma mater (a small Christian liberal arts college in Oklahoma City) offered me a new position. I was tasked with rebuilding an underperforming fundraising department as the Vice President for University Advancement. Once again, I was responsible for fixing something that was broken.

At the college, I realized I had a deep passion for higher education, so I decided to pursue a doctorate in education with a focus in university administration. My hope was to one day become a university president, but before that, God had other ideas.

In 2011, God came calling. I like to say He dragged me kicking and screaming into full-time ministry. Honestly, it was the last thing I wanted to do, and my wife, Michele, and I tried to convince God He picked the wrong guy, but the Lord can be very persistent.

For a short season, God let me build something! I helped to launch a campus for Victory Church in the Oklahoma City metroplex. During this time as a campus pastor, God gave me a second love—the local church. In fact, my affection for the church somehow surpassed the love I have for higher education.

Then, in 2014, my life got flipped upside down. Almost without notice, I went from campus pastor to lead pastor. Let me tell you how that happened.

The lead pastor of Victory Church had a moral failure. We were a 20-year-old multi-site church. The people were devastated, and the future dreams of the church seemed as though they were crushed. Our founding pastor was, and still is, a great man, but his mistakes caused massive trauma to a church that God had built.

My first reaction when I heard about the moral failure was that my days of ministry were over. I thought *Well, it's back to higher education for me*. But again, God had other plans, and before I knew it, the elders selected me as interim lead pastor.

Then, on November 2, 2014, I was named the lead pastor. To say I was in over my head was an understatement. At the time, I was only 35 years old with a meager three years of ministry experience. I had only preached a handful of times, and now I was expected to deliver a thought-provoking sermon almost every week. I had never led a team over five people, but now I had a staff of over 60.

Stepping into that level of leadership is difficult enough, but I had a few other difficulties staring me in the face. I had a shrinking congregation, which led to shrinking offerings. We needed money to minister to a hurting congregation that had just lost its shepherd. They had lost their trust in the church. A few had lost their faith. I also had a collection of staff members who needed help navigating through their own trauma left in the wake of the previous lead pastor.

So there I was, standing in the middle of the rubble, surrounded by pain and loss, trying to figure out how to fix what I had no hand in breaking. I was being called on to hold together and rebuild what was falling apart. I didn't have a name for what I was being tasked to do, but even then I *knew I wasn't being asked to lead—I was being asked to ReLead.*

Though it was excruciatingly difficult during this time, I fell in love with pastoring the local church. I'll lay out more of the gory details in chapters that follow, but after two years, the church was getting back to health and growth. I assumed my time in higher education was just a detour on the journey towards discovering God's true calling in my life.

Back when I was a campus pastor, I was ABD ("all but dissertation"), which means I had finished the coursework for my doctorate but not the dissertation. I had all but given up on getting my degree, but Michele would hear nothing of it. She began challenging me to finish. I would try to explain to her that I didn't need the degree to do what I was doing. I would respond to her, "But why would I finish it?" Then Michele would answer my objections with something that would pierce my argument and my soul: "Because you're not a quitter!" So I did what any wise husband would when his wife gives a challenging, inspiring, and convicting speech—I started drafting my dissertation.

In August 2017, I defended my dissertation and quietly got my doctorate degree. I didn't announce it at church, nor did I have people start calling me "Dr. Chasteen." I tried to get my wife to do it on our date nights, but I'll let you figure out the results. I only finished the degree because I am "not a quitter." Little did I know that God was setting me up for my next ReLeader assignment.

In late March 2018, my diploma arrived in the mail. Not even bothering to frame it, I simply set it to the side of the desk in my home office. Three weeks later, I was turned upside down again when I received a call from The King's University (TKU) in Southlake, Texas. The leadership asked if I would consider becoming their next president!

I was **floored**.

I was **confused**.

Franky, I was **borderline angry**. I thought, *God, I just found my groove in this lead pastor thing. I'm finally comfortable. Why would You disrupt me with this now?*

At first, I politely told the leaders at TKU that I was flattered, but (and I meant this with every fiber of my being) "I can't leave this church. We just got healthy. It took us four years to rebuild. I can't abandon this work!" In some ways, I felt like Nehemiah when he said, "The work is too important for me to come down off the wall" (see Nehemiah 6:3).

That's when the voice on the other end of the call said words I'll never forget: "We don't want you to leave Victory Church. We want you to do *both*."

I wanted to scream, "What? Are you insane?" Actually, I didn't ask that or scream, but I was screaming in my mind. So I hung up, feeling like I had been thrown onto that Tilt-A-Whirl ride at the traveling carnival set up in a field on the side of the road. I didn't know what to think, and I didn't know what God was up to.

And that's when a friend introduced me to **the God of *and*.**

Back in 2014, when our church had recently been punched in the gut, Craig Groeschel of Life.Church had called me. He said, "Jon, Oklahoma City needs Victory Church, and I will do everything in my power to help your church get through this." And that is what he did. Craig became a vital part of our church's survival, proving his love for the capital "C" Church. In the years that followed, he became one of the most influential people in my life. Craig has been my pastor and mentor as he helped to shape me into the leader I am today. In fact, I credit him with the title of this book.

By 2018, when I got the dizzying phone call from The King's University, Craig and I had formed a great relationship. Since he was my pastor, I had to tell him about this absolutely crazy new opportunity. We met at the gym for a quick workout, but my thoughts and fears soon spilled out of me. I asked him, "Craig, this is crazy, right? Can this be done? I can't lead a church *and* a university, at the same time, in two different states. Can I?"

I will never forget his response.

Craig sat up from the bench press—after pushing up some serious weight—turned around to me where I was standing in a spotter's position, and said, "Jon, you've never met the God of **and**. You've only met the God of **or**."

That's when the Tilt-A-Whirl instantly stopped.

I froze.

"Jon," Craig continued. "Sometimes God's calling is not either/or. Sometimes it's both/and. Of course, you can do it."

I was completely captivated by his words.

Craig went on: "Think about it this way, Jon. God entrusted me with Life.Church **and** the Craig Groeschel Leadership Podcast **and** the YouVersion Bible app **and** the Global Leadership Network. God entrusted Chris Hodges with Church of the Highlands **and** Highlands College **and** the ARC church planting organization." He continued, "Oh, and by the way, Jon, God gave the apostle Paul the Church of Corinth **and** the Church of Philippi **and** the Church of Thessalonica **and** the Church of Colossae."

I believe it was the voice of the Lord speaking through Craig when he continued, "Jon, this is just your next **and**. God has prepared you for it. You can do this. And I'll help you in any way I can."

On July 1, 2018, I started my new role as president of The King's University. What did I discover? Yep, it was a rebuild.

The King's University is a fully accredited higher education institution with a seminary. The school offers bachelor's, master's, and doctoral degrees in theology and ministry. It has quite a legacy. The school was founded in 1997 by a ministry legend, the late Jack Hayford. Sixteen years later, the school was moved to Southlake, Texas, where it is stewarded by Gateway Church. Pastor Jack was in the twilight years of his ministry. The university had survived some lean years before the move, so the transition was intended to be a shot in the arm to give life to the school, which may not have otherwise survived. Through the generosity of the church, the university became financially stable and debt free.

However, the internal state of the organization had become volatile, and the culture confused. I quickly realized I was leading an incredible organization, built from the foundations of Jack Hayford's incredible legacy and Christ Himself. It was no mistake that Pastor Jack chose to name it "The King's University." All the pieces were there, *but* we were going to have to put them back together.

Once again, God was calling me to ReLead.

YOUR RELEADING JOURNEY

I am a ReLeader.

My presupposition is that you are reading this book because God has also called *you* to ReLead in some capacity. It is a high calling! ReLeaders are essential in every aspect of life—in family, in business, in personal growth, and in health. But ReLeaders are particularly important to the local church. They are *needed.*

A 2021 study from Lifeway Research, based on data from over 30 denominations, discovered that 4,500 churches closed in 2019, while only 3,000 were started.[1] The 2021 Faith Communities Today study found the median worship attendance for churches in America dropped from 137 to 65 people over the past two decades.[2] I love church planting and support it both philosophically and financially. However, the current numbers of church plants are not keeping up with the amount of church closures. It seems abundantly clear that we must continue to build new churches, while not forsaking the importance of ReLeaders who are called to *re*build broken ones.

I have not mastered the art of ReLeadership, but I believe God has anointed me to lead in this capacity, and I know I've learned many indispensable lessons over the years. In this book, I'll share the best of what God has taught me.

I'm even more excited to give you a framework for ReLeading that I've discovered in the Bible. God provided us a powerful example of how to ReLead in the books of Ezra, Haggai, and Zechariah. After the Babylonian Exile, the Jews had to come back and rebuild what they didn't break. From this beautiful story of restoration and redemption, God gives us a blueprint for ReLeading:

1. *REspond*: God will stir your spirit with a spark of enthusiasm.
2. *REmember*: To move forward you must first look back.
3. *REquired*: We need to count the cost of what will be required to ReLead.
4. *REassurance*: Along the way, you will want to quit, but God will give you promises that will sustain you.
5. *REfocus*: Where do you start when it's time to rebuild? How do you refocus people behind the mission and recreate core values that will keep you moving in the right direction?
6. *REestablish*: To rebuild the foundation you must build trust, build people, and build systems.
7. *REmain*: You don't have what it takes. Your strength won't cut it. That stops many, but we will learn how to rely on God's grace to overcome.
8. *REbuild*: How do you rebuild something you've never seen? Through our guides Ezra and Haggai, God will teach us.
9. *REinforce*: What do you do next when you realize that when you're finished, you're not finished? We'll find out.

If you've been looking for a step-by-step process, then I have good news: You'll get one in the pages to come.

We are about to go on a journey, which I expect will be life-changing for you. And we are going to have fun along the way. Right now, I want to encourage you: You can rebuild it—whatever "it" is.

- You can rebuild your organization.
- You can rebuild your department.
- You can rebuild your marriage.
- You can rebuild your thinking.
- You can rebuild your finances.

With God's help, you can rebuild it, even if you didn't break it.

1

REspond

THE SPARK

I had no idea I was about to be ambushed by God.

But I was.

And it changed my life.

It was the summer of 2014. Our lead pastor's indiscretions had sent our church into a tailspin. I was young, had never been a lead pastor, and had only preached a few times. Still, Victory Church asked me to assume the role of interim lead pastor, and feeling like I couldn't tell them no, I said yes.

I was in way over my head, and I knew it.

It was a Friday evening a couple months later, and our church's young adult group was holding a worship night. I decided to step in to see how it was going. When I slipped in through the back door, the band was just beginning "Oceans" by Hillsong United. At the time, the song was still new, so I had only heard it a few times. The worship leader began to sing about trust without borders, walking on the waves, and how stepping out in faith will only make our faith stronger.

My intention was to do a brief check-in on our young adult ministry, but God had other ideas. The song continued, and I sensed the Holy Spirit whispering to my heart: "Over your head is where you belong. It's time to get away from the safety of the shoreline and go into the deep where there are sharks and waves. Do not fear—the only waves that will overtake you are the waves of grace that I will pour over you."

A switch flipped, and just like that, God changed my heart and mind.

Only a moment earlier, I was burdened by overwhelming dread at the intimidating challenge I was facing. Now I felt overwhelming excitement. God had infused me with a spark of enthusiasm.

A few pages from here in this book, and I will start to tell you about the rebuilding of the Temple in the book of Haggai. Its relevance to us today is startling. You will see clearly that the whole process begins with God calling two men to lead the work: "So the LORD sparked the enthusiasm of Zerubbabel ... and the enthusiasm of Jeshua" (Haggai 1:14 NLT).

If you're a ReLeader, then I'm guessing you've felt that spark. Why else would you have said yes to your leadership assignment?

Have you ever seen a building on fire as the fire department arrives? Everyone else is trying to get *away from* the burning building. Then a group of brave men and women show up and run *toward* what everyone else is running from. They run *into* the situation others are running out of.

That's a great picture of a ReLeader.

The severity of the fire will differ depending on the organization and the challenges it's been through, but if you're a ReLeader, you're willing to run in while others run away.

Why do you do it?

Because God called you to it.

Because He put within you a spark of enthusiasm.

If you don't sense that unique call from God to fix what is broken, then I would encourage you to walk away as soon as possible. You need that gift from the Holy Spirit because it will equip you with His empowering grace even during the most challenging times.

But since you picked up this book and are still reading, my bet is that God *has* sparked your enthusiasm to rebuild something. You're a ReLeader. In fact, can I encourage you to put this book down and take a moment to think back to when you were first called? When you're in the middle of a war, sometimes it's easy to forget what you're fighting for. Do you remember the still, small voice of the Spirit speaking to you? Do you recall that spark of enthusiasm you felt in your heart and mind?

I believe enthusiasm is essential.

The Hebrew word for enthusiasm is *ûr.*[1] It means 'to arouse, to awaken, to be stirred up and excited.'

Ûr is when you *know* God is calling you to ReLead. God sparked the enthusiasm of many:

- Moses led the children of Israel out of bondage.
- Noah built a boat.
- Elisha burned his plows and left everything to follow Elijah.
- David, a shepherd boy, faced a giant.
- Nehemiah rebuilt the wall.
- Twelve men left all they knew to follow Jesus.
- Paul endured trials, led the early church, and wrote over a quarter of the New Testament.

Anyone who's ever done anything significant for God first received the spark from God.

Anyone who's ever done anything significant for God first received the spark from God.

It's dangerous to ReLead without it. If you don't have the spark of enthusiasm, one of two things will happen:

- You won't finish the work.
- You will finish it but burn out in the process.

There is a process to ReLeading, and it starts with a spark.

I hope you've seen it in your life, and we're about to see it in the lives of two biblical ReLeaders, Zerubbabel and Jeshua, who ran into a fire others ran from.

ZERUBBABEL AND JESHUA

I was shocked when the leadership of Victory Church asked me to be the interim lead pastor, and I reluctantly said yes. But then I sensed God's calling as I listened to those Hillsong lyrics about having trust without borders and walking on water, wherever God might call me. So when I was asked to be the permanent lead pastor, I was ready. Well, I was not ready in the sense that I was prepared for the challenge. I wasn't even close to ready in that way. I was ready because God had foreshadowed this moment, and I knew it was from Him.

I said yes.

Then I thought ... *Now what?*

How do you fix something that is broken? Especially, how do you fix it when it's a complicated rebuilding situation with a convoluted history? I needed a plan, preferably a step-by-step strategy, and God gave me one.

Correction: God gave **us** one.

What Was Broken

King David was dead. That led, of course, to great sadness across the land. Even so, it was not all bad news for Israel.

David's son, Solomon, was chosen as the new king. He was wise and impressive. It was a promising time.

Then things got better. In the fourth year of his reign (see 1 Kings 6:1), Solomon began a huge construction project. He had enlisted the people to build a Temple for God in Jerusalem. This massive undertaking was launched with great fervor, and seven years later, it was complete (see 1 Kings 6:48). I probably shouldn't mention the fact that Solomon also built a mansion for himself, which took *13* years to complete. Nevertheless, the people finally had a permanent place to meet God.

In 1 Kings 8, the priests brought the Ark of the Covenant to the new Temple. Clouds representing God's presence filled the Temple, and then the whole Temple grounds were filled with fervent prayers, unrestrained praise, heartfelt dedication, and passionate celebration. The people did all these things because a Temple had *finally* been built for the God of Israel.

Four hundred years later the Temple, the city walls, and Solomon's fancy mansion were all completely destroyed.

The Babylonian army, led by King Nebuchadnezzar, conquered Jerusalem and burned the Temple to the ground.

> On August 14 of that year, which was the nineteenth year of King Nebuchadnezzar's reign, Nebuzaradan, the captain of the guard and an official of the Babylonian king, arrived in Jerusalem. He burned down the Temple of the LORD, the royal palace, and all the houses of Jerusalem. He destroyed all the important buildings in the city. Then he supervised the entire Babylonian army as they tore down the walls of Jerusalem on every side. Then Nebuzaradan, the captain of the guard, took as exiles the rest of the people who remained in the city, the defectors who had declared their allegiance to the king of Babylon, and the rest of the population. But the captain of the guard allowed some of the poorest people to stay behind to care for the vineyards and fields (2 Kings 25:8–12 NLT).

What had been a sign of God's great glory was set ablaze. The people thought of the Temple as the place where God's presence dwelled, but the Babylonians left nothing more than ashes.

And it was more than merely a Temple. It seemed as if God's people and their once great faith were also left in ruins. If God's house is in ashes, where is He going to live now—if He is still alive at all?

The Temple, and much of what it represented, was completely broken.

Something had to be done.

And someone had to do it. Someone must be willing to run into the fire rather than away from it.

Someone must be willing to run into the fire rather than away from it.

It turns out God had *two* someones—two ReLeaders—in mind.

The Call

> "The time has not yet come to rebuild the house of the LORD" (Haggai 1:2 NLT).

Years after the destruction of Jerusalem and its Temple, that's what God's people were saying.

I say they were God's people, but they weren't really acting like it. They weren't really prioritizing God at all.

Have you witnessed something like that? When something breaks—something like God's Temple in the Old Testament, or Victory Church in Oklahoma, or the organization you've been called to lead—it becomes easier for God's people to lose their focus on Him. Some people even start thinking, *After all, the whole God thing didn't go as planned.* And if people aren't exalting God, then they will usually exalt themselves.

That's exactly what was happening with God's people in the second year of the reign of Nebuchadnezzar's successor, King Darius. So God calls them out on it:

> "Why are you living in luxurious houses while my house lies in ruins?" (Haggai 1:4 NLT).

As it turns out, the people had become comfortable, and no one wanted to run back into the fire Nebuchadnezzar had started.

That's why they were proclaiming, "The time has not yet come to rebuild the house of the LORD" (v. 2 NLT).

Yes, that's what they were saying, but God had a different perspective:

> "This is what the LORD of Heaven's Armies says: Look at what's happening to you! Now go up into the hills, bring down timber, and rebuild my house" (Haggai 1:7–8 NLT).

It was time—time for God's people to rebuild God's Temple.

So how do you get people to do what they are *not* inclined to do?

Leadership. Or in the case of fixing something that is broken, *Re*Leadership. Through the prophet Haggai, God called Zerubbabel, who was a son of the governor of Judah, and Jeshua, who was a son of the high priest, to rebuild His house.

Zerubbabel and Jeshua were called to catch a vision. They were called to step up as ReLeaders to rebuild what they did not break. And watch what happens before anyone gets started:

> So the LORD sparked the enthusiasm of Zerubbabel son of Shealtiel, governor of Judah, and the enthusiasm of Jeshua son of Jehozadak, the high priest, and the enthusiasm of the whole remnant of God's people. They began to work on the house of their God, the LORD of Heaven's Armies (Haggai 1:14 NLT).

There it is. God sparked the enthusiasm of Zerubbabel and Jeshua.

To be a ReLeader, God will spark a desire within you to do something difficult that no one else wants to do. He will fill you with His *ûr*, which will then give you a sense of urgency.

The King James Version of this same passage says, "The LORD stirred up the Spirit" in Zerubbabel and Jeshua. It's the Lord who stirs this up in you. Without the Holy Spirit's empowerment, you will find it an impossible task, even for the most gifted of leaders.

Did you notice verse 14 *began* with God sparking their enthusiasm and *ended* with, "They began to work on the house of their God, the LORD of Heaven's Armies"?

Before the start came the spark.
God will spark you, but how will you REspond?

NOT ALONE

My family has a favorite show: *I Shouldn't Be Alive.* If you haven't seen it, it's fascinating. The show presents reenactments of true stories about people who faced impossible odds and survived to tell about it: stranded at sea, lost in the jungle, stuck in a snowstorm on top of a mountain, lived through an airplane crash, attacked by a lion, and dozens of other stories. These shocking scenarios of survival keep my family on the edge of our seats for an hour at a time. One thing we've noticed is the show's "alone" factor. Some face the threat of death with others while some face it by themselves. But those who face the hardship alone always have a harder time surviving the mental component of the ordeal.

On November 2, 2014, I was officially introduced as the new lead pastor of Victory Church. One week later, on November 9, I stood backstage before the beginning of the service and wondered if anyone had come back from the previous week. I remember thinking, *Our church has been through so much. Why would they stay? Wouldn't it be easier for them to find a church with less trauma and drama? And who am I? Why would they want to follow me?*

I can't forget the moment I opened the door and looked out over the auditorium. It was true that hundreds, if not more than a thousand, had left over the summer months after "the incident" and while I was interim. But as I looked, I saw *the remnant.*

That remnant was larger than those who had left, but it was a painful reminder of the trauma.

Every week for the next couple of years, I would walk toward the sanctuary, wondering if more had left and whether anyone had come back. And week after week, I was blown away at the faithfulness of the remnant.

Thinking back on the story of the rebuilding of the Temple, did you consider the fact that in Haggai 1:14, God didn't call Zerubbabel *or* Jeshua; He called Zerubbabel *and* Jeshua?

And did you notice Zerubbabel and Jeshua were not the only ones who responded to the spark? Haggai reported, "So the LORD sparked the enthusiasm of Zerubbabel ... **and** the enthusiasm of Jeshua ... **and** the enthusiasm of the whole remnant of God's people" (NLT, bold added).

I love that.

God never sends ReLeaders out on their own.

As I reflect on my journey, both at the church and the university, I realize I was never alone in my ReLeading assignments. Yes, many left during those difficult seasons of transition, but God surrounded me with a remnant who had received the same spark and who also responded to the call to rebuild.

At the church, God surrounded me with warriors like Dale Swanson, Wade Smith, Oscar Ortiz, Adam Fredrick, Steven and Sam Votaw, Jacque Parker, and hundreds of others whom God filled with the same enthusiasm to rebuild. At The King's University, God also surrounded me with faithful co-laborers who were committed to the cause.

As believers, we know we are not meant to do life alone. If you're a pastor like me, then you've made a statement like that, possibly many times. But I suspect we don't always live it out, especially in connection to our calling.

Is it time for you to acknowledge the remnant and focus on who still remains?

So, ReLeader, look around you. God has surrounded you with people who have the same spark that you received. Perhaps you could take a moment to thank God for them, and maybe reach out and express your gratitude to them?

If you feel alone, then what I wonder is if those people *are* there, but you haven't let them in or relied on them. Is it time for you to acknowledge the remnant and focus on who still remains?

NOT WHO HAS LEFT BUT WHO IS LEFT

The hardest part of my ReLeading journey was seeing people whom I loved leave. While I understood why they would respond that way to our lead pastor's moral failure, I couldn't help but feel a little betrayed.

It hurt.

I found myself constantly thinking of people I hadn't seen in weeks, adding them to the list of families who had walked out and would not return.

I felt like I was sinking into, and was afraid I'd settle into, the sadness.

Finally, God pierced my heart with a thought that would become almost a mantra for me: *ReLeaders learn to focus not on who has left but on who is left.*

It seems obvious, but when you're in a season of rebuilding, it's easy to become distracted by the many who are leaving.

300

The movie *300* is a fictionalized retelling of the Battle of Thermopylae in the Greco-Persian Wars. King Leonidas leads 300 Spartans into battle against the Persian army of over 300,000 soldiers. There are bizarre goat people and an army of immortal monsters, but the movie still has the kernel of a true history at its heart.

Over 600 years prior to the Battle of Thermopylae there is a completely true story from history, recorded in the book of Judges, and also featuring an undersized, outmatched army of 300. But much like the church I was called to pastor and the university I was called to lead, it started much larger.

If anyone understood the idea of a remnant, it was Gideon the judge.

In Judges 6, an angel of the Lord appeared to Gideon, who was threshing wheat at the bottom of a winepress. I'm no expert in wheat threshing or winemaking, but even I know wheat does not belong on the floor of a winepress. So why was Gideon doing his work in such a strange place? Most of the places used to prepare grain and food were demolished by the Midianites who are described as "enemy hordes, coming ... as thick as locusts; they arrived on droves of camels too numerous to count" (Judges 6:5 NLT).

Gideon is horrified by what has happened because of the Midianites and is hiding in the winepress trying to make the best of a bad situation when the angel shows up and greets him as "mighty hero" (Judges 6:12 NLT). I wonder if Gideon laughed. Gideon knew the one thing he was *not* was a mighty hero.

After Gideon's denial of his calling, the angel of the Lord commands him to "go with the strength you have" (Judges 6:14 NLT).

God saw Gideon's potential even before he did, and God sees yours too. Walking into your calling will always start with a willingness to engage with the strength God already gave you. But I'm not sure we can, or even should, say yes without the Spirit's spark of enthusiasm. That's what happens next with Gideon:

> Soon afterward the armies of Midian, Amalek, and the people of the east formed an alliance against Israel and crossed the Jordan, camping in the valley of Jezreel. Then the Spirit of the LORD clothed Gideon with power. He blew a ram's horn as a call to arms, and the men of the clan of Abiezer came to him. He also sent messengers throughout Manasseh, Asher, Zebulun, and Naphtali, summoning their warriors, and all of them responded (Judges 6:33–35 NLT).

Something came over Gideon that day. The Spirit of God did something for Gideon that is described as "clothed." I wear all kinds of clothes. Sometimes I have to dress up in suits, sometimes I wear swimsuits, but I really love a good pair of "stretchy pants." (Just think of the ones Jack Black wore in the movie *Nacho Libre*. I would like to think I get most of my fashion advice from *Nacho Libre*.) But of all the things we can be clothed with, God's power is at the top of the list. Clothed is translated from the Hebrew word *lāḇaš*. It means to 'put on, wrap around, or arm with.' Before this moment, Gideon was without God's power. But now it was on him, enveloping him, and arming him for battle.

After blowing the ram's horn and putting out the call to arms, an army of 32,000 men show up, ready to follow Gideon into battle. Then God says something that must have bewildered Gideon: "You have too many warriors with you." *Too many warriors? But the enemy has so many more. Why too many?* God explains: "If I let all of you fight the Midianites, the Israelites will boast to me that they saved themselves by their own strength" (Judges 7:2 NLT).

So God started giving Gideon instructions to whittle down the army. The Lord tells Gideon to say, "Whoever is timid or afraid may leave this mountain and go home" (v. 3 NLT). Like, "Fellas, if you don't have that spark, if you aren't clothed with power, then you can get to steppin'." At that point 22,000 of them leave! They were thinking to themselves, *Timid? Afraid? Yep, that's me!*—and they went home.

Now 10,000 are left who "were willing to fight" (v. 3 NLT), but God says, "There are still too many!" (v. 4 NLT) and gets rid of another 9,700.

Suddenly, there were just 300. No goat people, no immortal monsters, but just 300 men who felt the same spark of enthusiasm as Gideon.

Think about Gideon. Just days earlier, he would have been among the timid and afraid deserters. But because of the spark, he didn't even flinch when his army was reduced from 32,000 to 300. And that spark of enthusiasm, the undeniable power of God, caused that little army of 300 to rout those Midianites whose number of camels was described as like the "grains of sand on the seashore—too many to count!" (Judges 7:12 NLT).

The story of Gideon taught me that while the number of people who have left may seem significant, we should never underestimate the power of God or the enthusiasm of the remnant.

For Gideon, the remnant was *less than one percent* of his original fighting force. And our church lost several hundred, perhaps even a thousand people, but we were left with a lot more than one percent. I bet you were too.

Remember, ReLeaders learn to focus not on who has left but who is left.

Easier Said Than Done

Focusing on the remnant makes sense, but it's easier said than done.

Why is that so?

For me, when people left Victory Church, I couldn't help but feel like they were abandoning me.

I think an experience like that uncovers something in the heart of the ReLeader that must be dealt with before we can start rebuilding.

When people began to leave, it forced me to answer the question, *Why does this bother me so much?*

That's a challenge because it's difficult to be honest with ourselves, and the hardest person to lead is yourself. I realized, *I cannot respond to the calling to ReLead an organization without responding to the calling to ReLead myself.*

But here's the good news—the Holy Spirit comes alongside us in this process and starts a work in our hearts. If we let Him, He will carry it on to completion.

In fact, it was in those early years that God began to expose something in me that I could no longer ignore. I like to say we can never lead someone to a place *on* a stage that we haven't first visited *off* the stage. And it turned out God was about to lead me to a place off the stage that I was *not* excited to visit.

We can never lead someone to a place on *a stage that we haven't first visited* off *the stage.*

THE ORPHAN HEART

Have you ever had a personal problem, but you ignored it simply because you couldn't define it? Then something happened that brought clarity to the problem—and with clarity, perhaps increased pain—so you were finally able and willing to address it.

In my ReLeading journey, I came across the book *Called to Reign* by my now good friend Leif Hetland. This book defined what had been an inner battle that had been raging in me for years.

I had *an orphan heart.*

Consider how orphans think. These children have lost their parents and may find themselves in an orphanage. Perhaps one day the orphanage director tells the child that a family is visiting. If they dress right, act right, and speak right, then the family might just accept one of them and take them to their new home. They desperately want that to happen, and they realize the family's acceptance and love depends upon their behavior.

That thinking has to be at the core of every orphan.

There is an orphan heart in all of us—a deep desire to be liked, loved, and accepted.

So what happens when someone follows your leadership? You feel liked, loved, and accepted.

And then when someone leaves your leadership? It feels like the ultimate form of rejection. (And I know that feeling. In fact, in my first book, *Half the Battle,* I wrote a chapter on the damage and long-lasting impact of rejection.)

Remember the question I asked: *Why does it bother us so much when people leave?* Why do we focus so much on who *has* left instead of who *is* left? I think it's because it exposes our incessant need to be accepted. (Ouch! That hurts as much to type it out as it does to hear it!)

This may be an important God moment for you. It may bring clarity to a problem. So below the surface of your leadership, is there an orphan heart? Is something inside you crying out for acceptance and approval?

The good news is that we are in good company. As God exposed my orphan heart, He began to show me an orphan heart in many, if not most, of the Bible's major characters we've grown to love. Gideon had a massive orphan heart. That's why God's call for Gideon to become a ReLeader was met with self-doubt, self-loathing, anxiety, and fear.

The devil was the first orphan. He had been the worship leader of heaven. That seems like kind of a big deal. A resume with professional experience as "Heaven's Worship Leader" would probably get a lot of interviews. Think about it: The devil was once at home with our loving heavenly Father. But after trying to make himself equal to God, he was cast out of heaven. I wonder if he rebelled against God because of a desperate need for approval and affirmation. The devil left heaven, becoming the first orphan, and he's spent the rest of his life trying to make you feel just like he does.

Joseph's brothers had orphan hearts, which probably came as the result of their father loving Joseph more than them. That rejection led them to throw Joseph into a pit and then sell him into slavery.

Moses had an orphan heart—which may have been the result of being an actual orphan after his mother placed him in a basket in the Nile River, as well as experiencing rejection throughout his life. At the burning bush we see his orphan heart cry out with insecurity and fear.

Moses' brother, Aaron, had an orphan heart, which we see when Moses ascends the mountain to receive the Ten Commandments. Then Moses came down to find Aaron had made a golden calf for people to worship. When Moses questioned him, Aaron responds that he was afraid of the people, so he gave them what they wanted. Aaron's problem? He just wanted to be accepted.

King Saul had an orphan heart. When Samuel questioned him over why he had prematurely made a sacrifice to the Lord, Saul said, "I was afraid of the people and did what they demanded" (1 Samuel 15:24 NLT). Just like Aaron, Saul couldn't stand the thought of losing people's approval.

I think we see an orphan heart in Elijah. He experienced incredible victory when he called down fire from heaven on Mount Carmel, but a few verses later he is rejected by Jezebel. Elijah then prays and asks God to allow him to die.

Even the disciples had orphan hearts. Remember when they were arguing over who would sit next to Jesus in heaven? They craved recognition and desperately wanted to be valued.

The light bulb moment for me came when I read these words of Jesus in John 14, especially verse 18.

> "If you love me, keep my commands. And I will ask the Father, and he will give you another advocate to help you and be with you forever—the Spirit of truth. The world cannot accept him, because it neither sees him nor knows him. But you know him, for he lives with you and will be in you. I will not leave you as orphans; I will come to you" (vv. 15–18).

"Orphans" is translated from the Greek word *orphanos*, which means 'comfortless, those with no teacher, guide, or guardian.' An orphan is anyone who has no home or is looking for a place to belong. As Leif Hetland says, "Orphans have a longing for belonging."[2] I don't think Jesus chose *orphanos* by accident. I believe He used the word because He knew how susceptible we would be to the feeling of being comfortless and homeless, which could lead us to be so desperate for acceptance and approval that we might do things that are outside of God's will. These choices would be self-destructive and harmful to others.

Paul wrote about the actions of an orphan spirit:

> The mature children of God are those who are moved by the impulses of the Holy Spirit. And you did not receive the "spirit of religious duty," leading you back into the fear of *never being good enough*. But you have received the "Spirit of full acceptance," enfolding you into the family of God. And you will never feel orphaned, for as he rises up within us, our spirits join him in saying the words of tender affection, "Beloved Father!" (Romans 8:14–15 TPT).

I once heard a preacher tell the story of a dad who told his five-year-old, "Son, if all the five-year-old boys in the whole world were lined up in front of me and I could pick any of them I wanted, I'd choose you every time." He then asked his son, "If you could line up all the dads and pick any one you wanted, would you pick me?" The boy thought for a second and then said, "Well, I don't know. I'd have to see what the other dads had to offer."

If you have kids, many times do you find yourself asking, *How am I doing as a parent?* We constantly compare ourselves to other moms and dads and wonder how we're measuring up. But when was the last time you asked yourself, *How am I doing as a child of God?*

If God has called you as a ReLeader, then you must lead as a son or daughter, not an orphan.

A few years ago, I took my family to Mexico for vacation. In advance, I arranged and paid for transportation from the airport to the resort. We landed and walked out of the terminal as I had been instructed. The transportation company had told me to look for someone holding a sign with our last name (Chasteen) on it. When we exited, a sea of people were holding up signs, but we didn't see our name anywhere. I'm 6'7" so I had a good view, but no "Chasteen" was in sight. We waited and waited, but an hour later, still nothing. Finally, we got a taxi and forked over double the amount I had already paid for transportation.

A few days later, we had to pick up an itinerary and tickets for an upcoming excursion. At the top of the paper it said, "Reservations for John Castell." My first thought was, *Who is John Castell? Am I John Castell?*

Then it hit me. Back at the airport, my ride had been there all along! I probably walked right past the guy, but he was holding up a sign that said "Castell," and I was looking for one with "Chasteen." My ride was available—to take me to paradise—and I walked right by it because I was looking for the wrong name.

As you answer the call to ReLead and respond to the work God is laying out before you, make sure you answer to the right name. I wonder if God is standing on the sidelines of your life with a sign that says "Son" or "Daughter," and you're too busy looking for a sign that reads "Orphan." Maybe God's been calling you by a different name than the one with which you identify.

My advice to you, before you REspond to your calling as a ReLeader, is to make sure to confront your orphan heart. If you don't, your spark of enthusiasm could lead you to a forest fire where you will constantly try to win the approval of others.

God is a good Father, and before you fix what you didn't break in an organization, He wants to fix what's broken in you. Before He does a work *through* you, He wants to do a work *in* you.

Before He does a work through *you,*
He wants to do a work in *you.*

You cannot respond to the calling to ReLead an organization without responding to the calling to ReLead yourself.

2

REmember

WHAT DO YOU REMEMBER?

You've been there, right?

- You're taking a test, but you can't remember the answer!
- You need to remember your password, but no luck. Time to hunt for the password list.
- You've met this person several times before—you should know their name, but they walk up and the best you can come up with is, "Hiiii, how are you, friend?"

We often struggle to remember truly important things. But what's ironic is what we *can* remember. For example, depending on your age, I bet you can remember all the lyrics to the theme songs for *Gilligan's Island, Cheers*, or *Saved by the Bell.* Why is it that I don't know my wife's cell phone number but can recite every word of the *Fresh Prince of Bel Air* opening song by memory?

Have you ever considered how important remembering is to God? Depending on which Bible translation you use, the word *remember* shows up between 230 and 265 times, and the word *forget* appears between 60 and 75 times!

God repeatedly asks His people to remember. When the Israelites were about to walk into their Promised Land and begin to build, they were first told never to forget:

> The houses will be richly stocked with goods you did not produce. You will draw water from cisterns you did not dig, and you will eat

> from vineyards and olive trees you did not plant. When you have eaten your fill in this land, be careful not to forget the LORD, who rescued you from slavery in the land of Egypt (Deuteronomy 6:11–12 NLT).

And there are these other verses:

- "Remember the former things of old" (Isaiah 46:9 ESV).
- "Bless the LORD, O my soul, and forget not all His benefits" (Psalm 103:2 ESV).
- "I will remember the deeds of the LORD; yes, I will remember your wonders of old" (Psalm 77:11 ESV).

The night before His death, Jesus led His disciples through the Passover meal and instructed them, "Do this in remembrance of me" (Luke 22:19).

Jesus promised He would send the Holy Spirit after the Resurrection. One of the Spirit's greatest roles would be to "bring to your remembrance all that I have said to you" (John 14:26 ESV).

God keeps reminding us to remember, and I think it's because He knows how quickly and easily we forget.

We seem to have great memories for things like songs we haven't heard since high school. We will instantly sing along with them when they come on the radio. We can't seem to forget the hurtful things people said or did to us. We can remember never to eat at a certain restaurant again because of a bad experience we once had. We can recall exactly what we were doing on significant historical days in our lifetimes, such as the JFK assassination, 9/11, or January 6, 2021.

With all these memories, it's amazing how quickly we forget the goodness of God. In times of hardship, we quickly forget His faithfulness to us through the years. When we find ourselves in the wilderness, we're filled with fear, forgetting the manna He's always miraculously provided.

We forget, but God wants us to remember.

And remembering is essential when you step up to the call to become a ReLeader.

We forget, but God wants us to remember.

Before we rebuild, we need to remember.

BEFORE REBUILDING, THERE'S REMEMBERING

You just want to get started, right? Times have been tough. People are definitely frustrated, probably sad, and maybe despondent.

You have a vision for what's going to happen next, and the sooner you start, the sooner it will become reality. God has given you a spark of enthusiasm, and you are raring to go.

I get it. But you've got to be a little less fast and a little less furious. I know it feels like the best move is to jump right in and get moving, but this isn't a street racing action film. So, we're going to ignore our inner Vin Diesel and take our lead from God, who, as we will see, tells us to slow down before we start.

Why do we need to slow down? Because there's something we need to do first.

REmember.

Does Anyone REmember?

We can imagine how excited Zerubbabel, Jeshua, and all the people were to get started on the building of the Temple. And you would assume God would give them a joyous green light. After all, this was God's idea in the first place. But no. God takes Zerubbabel and Jeshua through one more step before they lift a tool. The Lord says,

> "Does anyone remember this house—this Temple—in its former splendor? How, in comparison, does it look to you now? It must seem like nothing at all!" (Haggai 2:3 NLT).

Before the people rebuild, God encourages them to remember. He recognizes that what once was, was no more. He acknowledges that what they were looking at must have seemed like nothing at all.

Why does God say this?

Before you can build something back, you need to look back and understand what was lost.

How Did It Look Before?

God asked, "Does anyone remember this house—this Temple—in its former splendor?"

When Solomon constructed the first Temple, it was one of the greatest structures ever built. Second Chronicles 2 and 1 Kings 5 give all the details, letting us know it included

- 3,600 supervisors,
- 70,000 enlisted laborers, and
- 80,000 men to quarry stone from the hill country.

First Kings 6 contains the extensive blueprints and the list of materials used for construction. And get this—they overlaid the entire inside with solid gold! Wow! In 1 Kings 7 we find out the Temple even had gold *hinges*, and 2 Chronicles 3 says they used gold *nails*. That's a whole other level! And each gold nail weighed 20 ounces. Today each of those nails would be worth over $30,000. And we can only guess how many nails they needed. In fact, there is quite a bit of speculation as to the cost of building the Temple. Most estimates place the cost of construction at somewhere between $100 and $300 million in today's value.

God asked if anyone remembered the former splendor of the Temple, and I think we can all agree it was incredibly spectacular.

Before you can build something back, you need to understand what was lost.

Today, when I walk the halls of our Victory Church campuses, I'm quickly reminded that I was not the original builder. Someone

- received a vision from God and led a group of people;
- sweat, bled, and sacrificed to do the work;
- developed leaders and hired staff; and
- worked with an architect and a contractor to build the foundation and structure I stand in today.

Regardless of mistakes made, or rubble that I'm now called to rebuild, someone came before me and did a good work for which I am grateful. I drink from a well that I did not dig and eat from vines I did not plant (see Deuteronomy 6:11).

That's the same with you, right?

When I became the lead pastor, I was tempted to forget the pain of the past and simply blaze a new trail. I wanted to rebuild but had no intention of looking at the original blueprints of the organization. The pain and rubble were so significant that my gut reaction was to focus only on what was lost and forget that there's also a legacy and a past.

If you're a ReLeader, you know what I mean by interim. Even if you are hired to take your role on a permanent basis, you know someone else will eventually follow in your footsteps. Whether it's for one year or 30, God's given you this role for just a season.

To know where to take your organization, you need to know where it's been.

We're in the now, and we want to be in the not yet. But first God wants to bring us back to what was. To know where to take your organization, you need to know where it's been.

HOW DOES IT LOOK NOW?

Have you ever seen before and after pictures?

I'm talking about the pics of people *before* they started their life-changing, "This is the one that will change everything!" diet and then *after* they've lost 60 pounds.

I've never taken one, but I've noticed the people in the before pictures always look pretty miserable. They're staring at the camera like, "Please, take me now. But before you do, destroy the camera."

I guess it makes sense that they look tragically unhappy. They're about to diet because they hate the way they look and feel, and now they have to take a picture highlighting and immortalizing that moment.

It seems almost like cruel and unusual punishment, except there's a reason for taking the before photo. There's something powerful about acknowledging where you are before you move forward.

In Haggai 2, God instructs the people to remember His former house in all its splendor and then asks, "How, in comparison, does it look to you now?" (v. 3 NLT).

After we remember what's been—in all its splendor—we need to take a good, hard look at what remains.

There's a scene in the movie *Titanic* where we see the great ship in all its magnitude and beauty. Then we watch as what remains slowly sinks to the bottom of the sea. Carry that even further, and people are still fascinated about the wreckage that sits on the ocean floor.

When God asks Zerubbabel and Jeshua to consider what remained, what is left is pathetic and paltry. Because His people repeatedly worshipped other gods, God sent King Nebuchadnezzar and his armies to turn what had been built to rubble.

Like many of the church systems, organizations, and dynasties we see today, what is built up is too often torn down.

I remember the moment so well. For nearly 20 years, Victory was one of the largest, most impactful churches in Oklahoma City.

Then, suddenly, this big ship crashed into an iceberg and was taking on water. I remember where I was when I first heard the news. As I was driving up to our Edmond church campus for an evening event, my cell phone rang. I was floored by the news. Three years in from leaving higher education, I now felt trapped. *I left a good career as a VP at a university, and now this,* I thought to myself. Little did I know in that moment that God would choose me to take the helm of this ship as it was taking on untold gallons of water. While I want this book to be an encouragement to you, I also need to be honest. ReLeading is difficult, and this was probably the lowest part of my journey. Think about it. Who in their right mind wants to take the helm of a ship that just struck an iceberg? It hadn't sunk yet, but it wasn't looking good. If I had known how difficult the following two years would be, I might have never agreed to put on the captain's hat. But this is what ReLeaders do. We have a calling to run toward what others run from.

"How, in comparison, does it look to you now?"

I bet Zerubbabel and Jeshua can relate, and if you're a ReLeader, you know what I'm talking about. *How in comparison does it look now? How in comparison does it look now?! What? Why?! Is God deliberately trying to make me depressed? God, You want me to remember its splendor, but look, the splendor is all splintered!*

And then there's what God says next: "It must seem like nothing at all" (Haggai 2:3 NLT). Though it may seem so, I don't think God is trying to bring discouragement. I believe He wants to bring understanding. He wants you to know that He knows.

The task in front of you seems impossible.

But He knows.

EVOLUTION, NOT REVOLUTION

Most leaders love change. Most people *don't.*

The majority of people in your organization like things the way they are. That's why they're a part of it; because they like what you do and how you do it. People also want to stay comfortable.

Leaders tend to be change agents, and it's easy to assume everyone feels the same. That's why most leaders want to present change as revolution: "We're going to do something totally new and different and exciting, and it's going to be great!"

The problem is that this terrifies most people. "No, thank you. You're messing with my comfort and with what I like."

When you present change as revolution, people will respond with fear and push back.

So, instead, we should present change as evolution.

Evolution is not a total departure from what we've always known, but a step forward based on our foundation. It is a step into the future, but with a connection to the past we've all experienced and enjoyed.

And to be clear, this is a better way of communicating change, but it's not disingenuous. There's always truth in the fact that a new initiative is birthed out of our institution's past. It's the same as fruit.

I love the thought that no matter what new fruit grows on a tree, it all started from the first seed planted. It's new fruit, proceeded from that same original seed. The fruit might look slightly different in shape or size, but it still came from the same place. And not only is there an apple in every apple seed, but there is also an *entire tree.* And not only is there a tree inside every apple seed, but there's also an *entire orchard* of potential.

ReLeaders do not see their roles as being revolutionaries who are called in to radically change everything the organization stood for in the past. Instead, they are called to guide the organization through evolutionary journeys, where they remember what God has done, and partner with those who have gone before them to allow God to use them to evolve the mission forward. The fruit might look slightly different than before, but the seed still remains.

I've learned, and now encourage you as a ReLeader, to find something in your organization's history to point to as an example of how you have *always* had a particular value.

Sometimes making that connection is easy. For instance, long before my time as lead pastor, Victory Church was referred to as "a hospital for the hurting." The church has always bused in people from homeless shelters and drug rehab homes on Sunday mornings. In Warr Acres, Oklahoma, where the original—and largest—campus is located, the median household income is $43,000 per year. Because of that, we have a largely blue-collar and beautifully diverse demographic. One of the new initiatives we launched in our rebuild was City Center. City Center is a non-profit organization we started across the street from our church that provides clothing, food, and mentorship to low-income families and students in the community. It was something new. Something we had never attempted. And so it was essential for us to help the people in the church see that it wasn't revolutionary; it was an extension of who we had always been, an evolutionary step straight out of the heart of our original purpose—to be a hospital for the hurting.

We started something new that we had never attempted before. To many it probably seemed like a distraction from the work we should be doing to recover from our brokenness. The truth is, to be a hospital for hurting people was at the very heart of our unchanging purpose. It was new fruit, but it grew out of our original seed.

I wish I could tell you I've always been so strategic and successful in presenting new initiatives, but the truth is I've made mistakes along the way. Pastor Jack Hayford started The King's University (TKU) with a heart to see the local church equipped and empowered by the Spirit to be change agents in the world. That was the seed of the seminary.

Shortly after arriving as the new president of TKU in the summer of 2018, I launched a project called "ChurchEd." I was excited. It was a very practical, much-needed resource for local churches to train their leaders for vocational ministry. Many churches hire talented individuals from within their congregations because they see leadership potential in them. Unfortunately, too often these individuals are very poorly equipped to do the practical work of day-to-day ministry. I know this is true because I was one of those people. In 2011, I left a job in higher education to become a campus pastor. While I was highly educated, I had zero experience in ministry. I was put in an office, given ordination papers, and told, "Welcome to the team, Pastor Jon." But I had no idea how to do weddings, funerals, stage time, pastoral care, or pretty much anything else ministers do. On my way to the hospital for my very first pastoral care visit, I Googled "What to say to someone who might be dying." (I'm not kidding.)

So, seven years later, ChurchEd was born.

ChurchEd was modeled after Master Class. It was designed as a fully online, inexpensive, high production quality product that allows pastors to receive training in very specific, niche areas in the church such as worship, youth, children's ministry, executive pastoring, audio/video, and pastoral care.

Great idea, right?

Yeah, I think so!

But when we first introduced the idea, it was *not* well received by many in our organization. To many it felt "beneath us" as an institution of higher learning. Some viewed it as a departure from our mission as a seminary. Why did they feel that way? I'm afraid it was because I introduced it as a revolution rather than an evolution. Because the truth is, it was *not* revolutionary; it was an evolution of the original dream of our founder, Jack Hayford, to train and equip the local church for ministry.

Don't make the same mistake. Find something in your history you can point to as an example of how you have *always* had this value. Point to the destination but show how it's just another step in a journey that started a long time ago. When we take this step, we're being faithful to our past and who we've always been.

HONOR'S REWARD

I've suggested there's something powerful about acknowledging where you are before you move toward where you're going, about walking through the past before you step into the future. Honestly, I've found there to be many rewards. One of the greatest benefits of this process is that it provides opportunities to honor those who have gone before you.

In my ReLeading journey I read a book by John Bevere called *Honor's Reward: How to Attract God's Favor and Blessing.* I highly recommend it. It helped me understand that not only is it right to honor your predecessors, but it also unlocks some pretty significant blessings.

There is a temptation that comes from taking over as the new leader. It is to *dis*honor those who have gone before us. You've been there, right? Often our first experience of them is the rubble they left for us to clean up. Instead of honoring, sometimes it's easier to dishonor.

There's a time we see Jesus in a very interesting predicament. We read, "He couldn't do any miracles among them except to place his hands on a few sick people and heal them" (Mark 6:5 NLT). Notice, it doesn't say He *wouldn't*—it says He *couldn't.* So what was it that restrained Him from doing miracles? I need to understand, because if I know what constrained Jesus, then I'll know what can constrain me. The answer is in the previous verses:

> Then they scoffed, "He's just a carpenter, the son of Mary and the brother of James, Joseph, Judas, and Simon. And his sisters live right here among us." They were deeply offended and refused to believe in him.
>
> Then Jesus told them, "A prophet is honored everywhere except in his own hometown and among his relatives and his own family" (Mark 6:3–4 NLT).

Jesus' hometown people were deeply offended, and it led them to dishonor Him. And their response born out of dishonor changed

Jesus' response to them. He could no longer do miracles among them.

The choice you make to honor or dishonor those who have gone before you will directly impact your ability or inability to ReLead.

The choice you make to honor or dishonor those who have gone before you will directly impact your ability or inability to ReLead.

When I became the lead pastor of Victory Church, Pastor Brady Boyd became an incredible mentor to me. Pastor Brady isn't just a leader; he's a true ReLeader. He was called to rebuild something he didn't break as the pastor of New Life Church in Colorado Springs, Colorado. He too stepped into a church on the heels of a moral failure by his predecessor, Pastor Ted Haggard. He understood my situation because he had walked a mile—or hundreds of miles—in my shoes. For the first several months of my new appointment, he would tell me repeatedly, "Jon, you honor the past every chance you get. Never miss an opportunity on stage to honor the legacy of those who have gone before you."

That is wise advice, but the temptation of ReLeading is to ignore it. The mistake the former leader made seems so painful and damaging that it's easy to reduce them to that mistake. We negate years of great leadership before the moment the Temple was torn down. If we do that, we miss a critical step in the remembering portion of our calling to rebuild.

I did what Pastor Brady told me. I honored our founding pastor from stage on a regular basis. I was well aware of what he had built and knew that one mistake didn't cancel all the good he had done in over 20 years of ministry.

Can I inspire you as Pastor Brady did for me? No matter how devastating the destruction of the Temple was, and how much rubble you're standing in, and how challenging a road you face, there is *always* a place for honor.

Even if you have a difficult time respecting the former leaders, you can honor them. My pastor, Craig Groeschel, says it this way: "Respect is earned. Honor is given." You do not have to respect someone to honor them. Think of it this way: In a theatrical play, the person who runs the spotlight at the back of the auditorium holds the power to highlight what everyone should look at during the production. As the ReLeader, *you* have control of the spotlight. We don't have to put the spotlight on the destruction; we can place it on the splendor of what was by honoring those who have gone before us.

At some point in your organization, there was a Nebuchadnezzar who came along and destroyed what had once been a house of splendor. But it should not stop you from honoring and respecting what once was. If you're a ReLeader, take your eye off the bad choices and introduce honor to the culture of your organization. You can never go wrong when you lead from a place of honor.

AN ASSIGNMENT

Can I give you an assignment?

Before you move on to the next chapter, *remember*.

You may need to find out more about the history of the organization or department you've been called to ReLead. Perhaps you can ask people who have gone before you or the remnant that remains for their perspective.

No matter the condition of the rubble you find yourself standing in, take time to remember and to honor.

It will help you not only look back but also get a more accurate picture of the future. And as we'll see in the next chapter, it's important for ReLeaders to know what will be required of us—in advance.

3

REquired

INSIDE THE LOCKER ROOM

I love locker rooms.

Actually, no. They usually have a funky foot smell, and there's nothing you want to see in there. Too much is wet. Too much is dirty. And too many people have fewer clothes on than I ever want to see. I *don't* love locker rooms. Let me start again.

I don't love locker rooms, but I do love locker room speeches.

Not the generic, "Hey, guys, remember what we've practiced. Let's go get 'em!" speeches.

No, I'm a fan of the "We're about to face the biggest challenge of our lives, and no one thinks we can win, but we're gonna do this!" locker room speech.

Everywhere I go, people look at me and say, "You're tall." (Please don't tell tall people they're tall—they already know). So it should come as no surprise that I was obsessed with basketball growing up and went on to play college basketball for four years. As such, I've heard my fair share of locker room speeches. One of the best ones I ever heard was a halftime speech. Mark Arthur, my college coach for four years, lit a fire under us that night. We were losing to a team we had no business losing to. Normally, Coach Arthur was an incredibly even-tempered leader, but this night he came in, threw a chair, and might have said a few choice words not normally heard at a Christian university. Something about his passion lit us up—and it worked. We came out and had one of our greatest comebacks.

If you've never personally experienced a locker room speech, then you've probably seen one in a sports movie. Here are a couple of my favorites:

In the movie *Miracle*, Kurt Russell, playing USA Olympic hockey coach Herb Brooks, gives a locker room speech before his team takes the ice against the juggernaut Soviet Union squad. He challenges his team with focused intensity:

> Great moments are born from great opportunity. And that's what you have here tonight, boys. That's what you've earned here tonight. One game. If we played 'em 10 times, they might win nine. But not this game. Not tonight. Tonight, we skate with them. Tonight, we stay with them. And we shut them down because we can! Tonight, *we* are the greatest hockey team in the world. You were born to be hockey players. Every one of you. And you were meant to be here tonight. This is your time. Their time is done. It's over. I'm sick and tired of hearing about what a great hockey team the Soviets have. This is your time. Now go out there and take it.

And then there's Coach Dale in *Hoosiers*, inspiring his small-town basketball team before the state semifinal game:

> And most important, don't get caught up thinking about winning or losing this game. If you put your effort and concentration into playing to your potential, to be the best that you can be, I don't care what the scoreboard says at the end of the game. In my book, we're gonna be winners. Okay?

And then starts the infamous slow clap, which soon becomes thunderous, with the players shouting, "Let's go! Let's go!"

They win, and so we watch as they prepare for the state championship, in which they are given no chance. Before the game, instead of a speech, Coach Dale has a pastor speak. He steps up and says, "And David put his hand in the bag and took out a stone, slung it, and struck the Philistine on the head, and he fell to the ground. Amen."

One more? It's not quite a "locker room" speech, but it might be the most inspiring "pregame" pep talk I've heard. If you're a guy and don't know this speech, you will have your man card revoked immediately. *Braveheart* is one of the top five movies ever made (don't you dare challenge me on that). Before riding out on the battlefield, William Wallace, with his war-painted face, shouted,

> Aye, fight and you may die. Run and you'll live, at least a while. And dying in your beds many years from now, would you be willing to trade all the days from this day to that for one chance, just one chance to come back here and tell our enemies that they may take our lives, but they'll never take our freedom!

Where's my sword? Those words make me want to fight for his guy!

Why are these motivational speeches necessary? Because the players are about to engage in what seems an impossible challenge. It will be *hard* for them to accomplish their goal. So their leader says something like, "Here's what will be required of you. Now let's go do it."

Remember, God called Zerubbabel and Jeshua to lead like-minded Israelites in the rebuilding the Temple. God ignited the process with that call. Then we saw God have the people look back and remember. Now you would think it's finally time to start the work. But not quite yet. First, God had to give them the locker room speech.

> *You've been called. The Spirit has given you the spark of enthusiasm. Now, you need to understand what will be required of you. Great moments are born from great opportunity. You were meant to be here. Put all your effort and concentration into this. Now let's go do it.*

We find the first part of the actual speech in Haggai 2:4–5:

> "But now the Lord says: 'Be strong, Zerubbabel. Be strong, Jeshua son of Jehozadak, the high priest. Be strong, all you people still left in the land. And now get to work, for I am with you, says the Lord of

> Heaven's Armies. My Spirit remains among you, just as I promised when you came out of Egypt. So do not be afraid'" (NLT).

God basically makes four statements. We find Him saying these same four things throughout the Bible, and I'm convinced anyone who's ever been called to do anything great for God has heard the same message:

- Be strong.
- I am with you.
- Do not be afraid.
- Now go!

Why does God repeatedly give this speech?

- God tells us to be strong because He knows we'll feel weak.
- He tells us He will be with us because He knows we will feel alone.
- God tells us not to fear because He knows we have reason to be afraid.
- He tells us to go because He knows we'll be tempted to stay.

From Gideon in the wine press, to Moses at the burning bush, to Joshua on the banks of the Jordan River, to Jonah in the belly of a great fish, we see the same message throughout Scripture, and *you've* heard it if you've been called by God. He is saying to you: Be strong. I am with you. Do not be afraid. Now go!

He is saying to you: Be strong.
I am with you. Do not be afraid. Now go!

ReLeaders Do Hard Things

A few days ago, I had a conversation with my kids. As I write this book, they are in their early teens. It's the age when you teach them because they're getting closer and closer to stepping out into the world of "adulting." It is the age when, as a parent, you only have a few short years left to give instructions on how to survive outside the nest, and you're not sure you've done what is needed. (Help me, Jesus.) So what did I do?

I gave them a locker room speech.

It went something like this:

> If you ever want to do something great in this world for Jesus, and if you want to have any measure of success in this life, you will only do it by embracing the pain of doing hard things. No one is coming to do it for you. Find what God is calling you to do, count the costs of the sacrifice it will take, and go do it. If it is hard, chances are you're heading in the right direction.

Then I said something which has come out of my mouth hundreds of times. It's something I've told countless people throughout my years of leadership and now challenge my kids with it: "If it were easy, everyone would do it."

The issue is that everything in the world is trying to make our lives easy. You can now

- make your Amazon Prime purchases with one click;
- order your groceries online and have them delivered to you;
- wire money to someone through your phone, instead of having to write a check and put it in an envelope;
- get ready-to-make meals delivered to your home so you don't have to cut those peppers or dice those onions; and
- use a phone app to start and stop your washer and dryer, vacuum, or car.

I don't want to sound like the "Get off my lawn" guy, but our culture continues to cry out for the easy and wants to avoid hard work at all costs. "Healthcare should be free." "The government should pay off my student loans."

People today expect minimal work with maximum returns.

Yet God tells us not to fear and to be strong because He knows that what we're about to do will be *hard.*

If you're called to be a ReLeader for the Kingdom of God, then God saw something in you. If it were easy, then everyone would do it, but it's not. God knew *you* could do something others wouldn't be willing or able to do. You were born for this.

God knew you *could do something others wouldn't be willing or able to do.*

Put in all your effort and give all your concentration, knowing God is with you.

It may be painful, but pain heals.

(Start a slow clap here.)

This is your time. Now go! Take it!

MOVEMENT WITHOUT MIRACLES

Here's a great question: Why can't God do the hard things for us?

I mean, He's capable. Right? So why doesn't He just do it? God's unique specialty is *miracles.* We love the accounts in the Bible where God shows up and shows off. We enjoy sermons that promise God will swoop in and save the day.

So if the odds are stacked against our rebuild, why doesn't God just step in and do His thing?

The answer is—I don't know.

But I *do* know that when it comes to our calling and to advancing the Kingdom of Jesus, we are soldiers in the army of God, and as such, we show up ready to do hard things. Sometimes God protects us from hard things, but most of the time He chooses to give us the tools and the strength to get through them. In my life:

- God does not usually part the waters in front of me. Instead, He provides the wisdom and strength to build a boat.
- He doesn't take me out of the lion's den, but He does shut the mouths of the lions.
- He doesn't extinguish the fiery furnace, but He goes into the fire with me to protect me from the flames.

I also know that sometimes we get miracle stories with no miracle. But I wonder if maybe, in a sense, the miracle *is* the hard work. One of my favorite stories in the Bible is a perfect example.

The Miracle Story with No Miracle

Spoiler alert: Zerubbabel and Jeshua *do* eventually rebuild the Temple. Our story will have a great ending. We'll see that later, but right now we need to jump in a time machine to about 70 years after their work is complete.

It was necessary to rebuild the Temple because King Nebuchadnezzar and the Babylonians had invaded and ransacked Jerusalem. After burning down the Temple, "he supervised the entire Babylonian army as they tore down the walls of Jerusalem on every side" (2 Kings 25:10 NLT).

The walls were essential to protect the city and its citizens from foreign invaders. Eventually, as we're learning, some Israelites were led back to Jerusalem to rebuild the Temple, but the walls of the city still remained in a heap. For 70 more years there were no walls to guard the city.

Nehemiah heard about the situation, and it broke his heart. It gave him a spark of enthusiasm. He felt compelled to lead a rebuilding effort—and he did.

Why do I call it a "miracle story with no miracles involved"? Because they rebuilt the walls in 52 days. The Temple had been rebuilt but left unprotected for 70 years. Then they rebuilt the walls in only 52 days!

So why hadn't anyone else attempted to rebuild the walls? Because if it were easy, everyone would do it. But it was not easy, and God wasn't going to intervene with an instantaneous, microwaved miracle. The leaders in Jerusalem were also afraid building the walls would look to their enemies like they were once again becoming an independent nation. Fear of hard work and fear of their potential enemies kept the people from doing anything at all with the city walls.

So God simply sent common, ordinary people to step up and rebuild what had been broken. The miracle was fleshed out in the day-to-day grind of God's people doing God's work even though it was hard and even though they may have felt fear. Please understand, as a ReLeader, it's very likely your journey to rebuild will look just like that.

Concern

How do we know when God has called us to be involved in a ReLeadership opportunity? I would tell you that God's calling starts with a deep concern for something that is broken.

- What causes a woman to start a nonprofit for single moms? A concern.
- What causes a man to make his family a priority over a career? It's his concern for ensuring his kids are raised to serve Jesus.
- What caused the apostle Paul to passionately lead the early churches? Paul said, "Besides everything else, I face daily the pressure of *my concern for all the churches*" (2 Corinthians 11:28, italics added).

Why did Nehemiah answer the call? *Concern.* Concern is the seed God plants in your heart that compels you to say yes. We see this concern as part of Nehemiah's calling:

> They said to me, "Those who survived the exile and are back in the province are in great trouble and disgrace. The wall of Jerusalem is

> broken down, and its gates have been burned with fire." When I heard these things, I sat down and wept (Nehemiah 1:3–4).

Nehemiah responded to God's call to be a ReLeader and fix what someone else had broken.

> I went to Jerusalem, and after staying there three days I set out during the night with a few others. I had not told anyone what my God had put in my heart to do for Jerusalem (Nehemiah 2:11–12).

However, before God placed the seed in his heart, and before he responded to the call, Nehemiah was concerned. Concern gives you a sense of urgency that spurs you on to do hard things:

- If you are concerned about your health, then it might compel you to start working out and eating right.
- If you are concerned about your marriage, then it might compel you to go to counseling.
- If you are concerned about your finances, then it might compel you to get on a budget.
- If you are concerned about your future, then it might compel you to go back to college and get an advanced degree.

If you are currently in a ReLeader role and your passion seems to be fading, then try to find the concern that once sparked your enthusiasm.

Where is your current level of concern? When you think of what is broken, does your heart break? Are you tempted, like Nehemiah, to sit down and weep? Or is it possible your concern has been somewhat quenched with time? If so, do you remember how your heart used to beat fast? Do you recall nights when you lost sleep because of your passion for what God had called you to do?

If you're trying to decide whether or not to take a new ReLeader role in an organization, make sure the brokenness in front of you brings concern to your heart that is big enough for you to want to respond to it.

If you are currently in a ReLeader role and your passion seems to be fading, then try to find the concern that once sparked your enthusiasm.

WHAT TO EXPECT WHEN YOU'RE RELEADING

The book *What to Expect When You're Expecting* is a guide for expectant mothers. It first came out in 1984 and has become a mega-best seller. If you're experiencing your first pregnancy, then it's a huge help to know what you can expect, and that book provides advice on how to handle the mood roller coaster, the physical symptoms you'll experience, and much more.

As a man, and therefore someone who will never experience pregnancy, I'm a bigger fan of *The Worst-Case Scenario Handbook.* Have you seen it? It gives simple steps to survive some of life's worst situations. In that book you will learn how to deliver a baby in a taxi, wrestle free from an alligator, jump from a moving car, and avoid being struck by lightning. Have you ever wondered how to survive if your parachute doesn't open? Here it is:

- Step One: Signal to a jumping companion whose chute has not yet opened that there is a problem.
- Step Two: While traveling at 130 miles per hour, hook arms with your companion.
- Step Three: Open the chute (this will probably dislocate or break your arms).
- Step Four: If there is a body of water nearby, head for that.[1]

Those instructions don't fill me with confidence. I'm not sure I would be able to signal a companion or hook arms with them. I'm also not optimistic about my ability to head for water with broken arms.

There is no book called *What to Expect When the Worst-Case Scenarios You Weren't Expecting as a ReLeader Start Happening Handbook*, but maybe there should be.

In the book of Nehemiah, we get to see the challenges Nehemiah faced, which gives us great insight into the playbook of our enemy.

Here are *Five Things to Expect that Are Normal-Case Scenarios When You Do Hard Things as a ReLeader.*

1. Expect Trouble

Once your concern has led you to answer the call, there will be a threat to your success. The thing that can keep *us* from taking the risk of saying yes and making bold moves is *conflict,* such as the conflict that arose when Nehemiah raised the wall. I bet you've experienced some conflict yourself. Conflict or the fear of it can keep you from

- holding people on your team accountable;
- firing an employee even though everyone in the organization knows it needs to happen; or
- having the difficult conversation you know is necessary.

I wonder if conflict is holding you back from doing the hard things necessary to live out your calling. Where might that be true? I don't know your situation, but I do know your concern *will* lead to conflict. I know that's not very encouraging, but it's true. So don't dread it; expect it. Because if you expect it, then you can plan for it.

Anything worth building becomes a target to the enemy. If you decide to

- rebuild your marriage,
- raise godly kids, or
- build your business with godly values,

then the devil will take notice. And he will start shooting fiery arrows at what you're dreaming about and working on.

Nehemiah made the decision to rebuild something important, and the enemy took notice.

> So we rebuilt the wall till all of it reached half its height, for the people worked with all their heart.
>
> But when Sanballat, Tobiah, the Arabs, the Ammonites and the people of Ashdod heard that the repairs to Jerusalem's walls had gone ahead and that the gaps were being closed, they were very angry. They **all plotted together** to come and fight against Jerusalem and **stir up trouble** against it (Nehemiah 4:6–8, bold added).

They worked "with all their heart," or as the NKJV reads, "for the people had a mind to work." They were committed to doing whatever it took. And doing hard things for the Kingdom of God caused the enemy to take notice and "stir up trouble."

The reason Nebuchadnezzar and his armies tore the walls down originally was because the walls were important. As a ReLeader, you need to understand that you're rebuilding something the enemy did not want to stand. He went to the trouble of attacking it, and now you're trying to build it back up. You better expect trouble.

My son and I love deep sea fishing, and we go nearly every summer. Actually, I don't love fishing; I love *catching fish*. Standing for hours with a pole in my hand is about as torturous as it gets for me. But we typically go on a private tour boat, and the guide knows the best places to catch fish. So usually within a few minutes we're pulling up red snapper, king mackerel, triggerfish, and whatever else is lurking down there. I know we're in a great "honey hole" spot when I reel in a catch and find only the head left on the hook. Yep, you know you've found the perfect fishing spot because the sharks show up.

As a ReLeader, you know you're rebuilding something worthy of your hard work when the sharks show up. It might feel nice if the going is easy and you're not facing any opposition, but I would consider that a warning sign that what you're doing is not eternally significant. Expect attacks—which will help you prepare in advance.

As a ReLeader, you know you're rebuilding something worthy of your hard work when the sharks show up.

When Nehemiah faced resistance, he took action. What did he do? "We prayed to our God and posted a guard day and night to meet this threat" (Nehemiah 4:9). I would vote for "and" as the most important word in that passage. They prayed *and* posted. Nehemiah tapped into God's supernatural power *and* did everything in his power in the natural. ReLeaders know the importance of doing *both*. We've heard the saying, "Pray like everything depends on God. Work like everything depends on you." Too often we do one or the other. We call a 24-hour prayer meeting, fast for weeks, and wait for God to move while we sit back and do nothing. Or we just give God lip service while we work ourselves into the ground trying to do it ourselves. Nehemiah did *both*. Nehemiah would tell us to do all these things:

- Pray for your sickness *and* go to the doctor.
- Pray for a new career *and* go back to school and finish the degree.
- Pray your marriage will be healed *and* serve your spouse selflessly.
- Pray for your mental health to be restored *and* go to a counselor.

As you step into your role as a ReLeader, expect trouble. The worst-case scenario probably will happen, but you'll be prepared to meet it with prayer *and* hard work.

In your ReLeader journey, one of the most troublesome aspects of your calling will most likely involve navigating your organization or department through financial challenges. This was by far one of my biggest pain points at Victory Church. When I became the lead pastor, the church was experiencing a significant decline in attendance, which in turn caused a significant decline in income. Even those who stayed had lost some measure of trust in the church, which never has a positive effect on giving. What did *not* decline were the expenses. Between the mortgage debt, payroll, and day-to-day operations, we were facing some challenging times. For me to pray and do nothing would be foolish. For me to do all I could but not pray would be equally unwise. So I decided to do what Nehemiah did. I prayed *and* worked. You know what God did not do? He did not send a dump truck filled with cash to fix all my problems. We focused on stewardship. We cut every possible expense. We established a new core value: "We steward God's resources well and with radical generosity." We changed the way our church talked, which changed the way our church behaved. No miracles, just a group called by God to ReLead, and thus rebuild a great church. We prayed like it depended on God and worked like it depended on us.

If you're a ReLeader, you should expect trouble, but you should also expect to overcome it.

Remember, if it were easy, everyone would do it.

2. Expect Exhaustion

Sorry, I know this isn't getting more encouraging, but you also need to expect exhaustion. Because, again, if we know what to expect, then we can be prepared to overcome the challenges when they arrive.

How do I know you'll experience exhaustion? Because doing hard things requires hard work. *Always.* It's what happened to the people of Judah when they followed Nehemiah's leadership in rebuilding the wall: "Meanwhile, the people in Judah said, 'The strength of the laborers is giving out, and there is so much rubble that we cannot rebuild the wall'" (Nehemiah 4:10).

You will reach a point during your rebuilding journey when you feel like your strength is giving out. If it hasn't happened yet, then you're on the clock.

The wall workers were standing in rubble, which was making it difficult to rebuild and was tiring them out physically. You probably get that. You may be working long hours and feel physically drained.

Many times in my ReLeader journey I reached this point. I can't tell you the number of times I sat alone and felt tears stream down my face or cried with my leadership team. I remember one particular time I was mowing my yard and feeling completely overwhelmed, like I was standing knee deep in rubble and couldn't figure out my next step. I parked the mower behind a tree so if my family looked out the window they wouldn't see me, and I started bawling like a child. Luckily, it was a hot day so my tears could be masked as sweat.

Nearly every time I reached a moment like this, I would receive a phone call from Jimmy Evans. Even on the mower that day, I looked down through my blurred, tear-filled eyes to see an incoming call from Jimmy Evans on the screen. The spiritual giants God put around me helped me push through in my darkest moments. When you find yourself in a pit of despair, you too will need spiritual giants to encourage and lift you up.

When you find yourself in a pit of despair, you too will need spiritual giants to encourage and lift you up.

But I don't think it's hard work alone that pushes ReLeaders to the edge. There's something even more exhausting. It's the third thing you should expect.

3. Expect a Mental Battle

The hard work of ReLeading can deplete your mental health. You've experienced it, right? You started ReLeading, and maybe for the first time, you began to struggle with depression or nearly debilitating anxiety.

Did you notice in Nehemiah 4:6 we're told they were working with all their heart and that the wall had reached half its height, and *then* the problems began. *That* tends to be when the enemy goes into overdrive and ramps up his plot to stop the work—at the halfway point.

Isn't that the way it goes? At the beginning there's excitement and renewed hope. Toward the end people see the results and are encouraged. But in the middle, you experience the perfect storm of mental, physical, and emotional fatigue. In the middle, burnout happens.

We get more insight into what was causing their exhaustion a few verses later:

> Also our enemies said, "Before they know it or see us, we will be right there among them and will *kill them* and *put an end to the work.*"
>
> Then the Jews who lived near them came and told us ten times over, "Wherever you turn, they will attack us" (Nehemiah 4:11–12, italics added).

We grow tired not only because of what our hands and feet do but also because of what our enemy says. Your enemy loves to deceive you and will constantly whisper "what ifs" in your ear. He works in worst-case scenarios the way Picasso worked in paint and DJ Jazzy Jeff worked the turntables.

My vote is that mental health issues are the most debilitating and dangerous. If we only struggled with physical exhaustion, we could take a nap. (Maybe *lots* of naps.) But when what you're facing is mental, not physical, a nap won't fix it. You'll probably wake up more tired than when you first laid down.

When I was in low moments in my ReLeading journey, I found I could rest my feet, but my mind was a different story. My body would lie still in bed every evening, but my mind was racing, playing out each worst-case scenario:

- I was concerned about the finances of the church.
- I thought about the 60-plus people depending on our church for a paycheck to put food on their tables.
- I had critical decisions to make week after week after week with our finances, staffing, facilities, vision, and direction of the church.
- I was trying to get into the rhythm of preaching every weekend.
- I was navigating pastoring a huge, hurting church.

My mind churned: *How do I provide pastoral care for thousands of people, be a discerning leader for the organization, bring a brilliant sermon every week, and somehow keep being a perfect husband and father? Oh, and I have to keep an intimate relationship with God as the central component of my life.*

It's no wonder pastors are burning out left and right. The Barna Group has uncovered some staggering statistics about the well-being of pastors in America in the last few years.[2]

- According to a November 2021 study, 38 percent of pastors have considered quitting full-time ministry. This percentage is up a full nine points from the beginning of 2021 (when it was 29 percent). Among pastors under 45 years old, the number climbs to 46 percent considering quitting, compared to 34 percent of pastors 45 and older.
- The same study revealed that only 35 percent of pastors consider themselves "healthy" in terms of their well-being.

I think it's safe to say that the "strength of the laborers is giving out," and the wall has still only reached half its intended height.

Here's the good news: If you're reading this, then you're not done yet! You've led through one of the most difficult times in modern history, and here you stand. God woke you up this morning and put breath in your lungs, which means He still has important work for you to do.

With God's help you've fought through some tough times, and now that you're through them, you should expect—and plan for—more to come. It's essential to be prepared in advance. We see that with Nehemiah, whose response was swift. He reports, "Therefore I *stationed some of the people* behind *the lowest points of the wall at the exposed places,* posting them by families, with their swords, spears and bows" (Nehemiah 4:13, italics added).

Nehemiah recognized his people were exhausted and did a quick analysis to discover the weakest points. He answered the question, *If the enemy is going to get through our defensive lines, where are we most vulnerable?*

Perhaps this is a great place for us to start:

- If the enemy is going to attack us, then where is he most likely to succeed? What are the weak spots in our organization?
- When I'm tired, where am I most susceptible? Am I tempted to pop a bottle or a pill? To go to a website I would not otherwise visit? To rationalize overeating unhealthy food as my reward for a hard day of work?

We need to answer those questions.

Regardless of your particular weak spot, there's one defense that is universally essential for all of us: *Rest.* We work hard, and so we must rest hard. But depending on your personality, the hardest thing you may ever have to do is make yourself rest.

Resting doesn't sound difficult. Its name would lead you to believe it's easy. But, again, if it were easy, everyone would do it. So many leaders *don't.* They neglect the Sabbath. They even boast about their overloaded to-do lists and how little sleep they get. *We're storming the castle! We're taking no prisoners! We don't have time to rest!* If only God agreed. And if only leaders who live like this finished well, but so many don't.

German theologian Gerhard von Rad said, "Among the many benefits offered to man by holy scripture, rest is the most overlooked." I think he's on to something. We're ignoring one of God's greatest gifts to us. Jesus said, "The Sabbath was made for man, not man for the Sabbath" (Mark 2:27). God created the Sabbath to give to us as a gift! Sadly, it's a blessing that few of us receive.

Here is *when* God created the Sabbath for us:

> Thus the heavens and the earth were completed in all their vast array.
>
> By the seventh day God had finished the work he had been doing; so on the seventh day he rested from all his work. *Then God blessed the seventh day and made it holy,* because on it he rested from all the work of creating that he had done (Genesis 2:1–3, italics added)

I've read and heard that passage hundreds of times, but I don't think I ever noticed that God *only* blessed the seventh day and only made *that* day holy. There were six other days, which were the days God did all the work of creation, but God did not bless them or make them holy. Only the seventh day. Why did He do that? "Because on it he rested from all the work of creating that he had done."

Now imagine all the work you do. You've been called to ReLead, and you are working your tail off to do it. It's hard work, and God honors that. But if God hasn't changed since the beginning, then the one day He will bless and make holy is the day you *rest*.

Think about that.

And what if you're not taking a day of rest?!

We need to be strategic about our Sabbath, intentional about resting. I love what Rick Warren said: "To avoid burnout, divert daily (whatever relaxes), withdraw weekly (a Sabbath), and abandon annually (disconnect completely)."[3]

When you take Sabbath seriously, you discover that it's medicine to a disease running rampant in our society called "striving." Our culture honors achievement, speed, progress, and busyness. It's the water we swim in. But striving is antithetical to life in God's Kingdom. Jesus taught us that we don't strive to produce fruit. He said He is the vine and we are the branches, and we produce fruit by simply remaining in Him. Walk through a garden, and you will not hear a branch groaning as it fights to form fruit. It produces fruit not through striving but through connection.

We need to be strategic about our Sabbath, intentional about resting.

We need to learn to pray,

> Return to your rest, my soul,
> for the LORD has been good to you (Psalm 116:7).

As we do, we'll realize that Sabbath has a rhythm. When you listen to music, you rarely notice the moments of silence. Your ear is focused on the things happening in the song, not on what's not happening. But any musical artist knows that silence is just as important as sound. Mozart said, "The music is not in the notes, but in the silence between." Silence provides relief and builds suspense. Without it, music would lose its meaning.

You cannot make music without rest.

The same is true in your life.

God is sovereign. With divine design He is writing the music of our lives, and He will *always* include rest. If we omit rest, we mess with His melody and tell Him that we want to write our own song on our own terms. There is a melody to your life, and your honoring the Sabbath creates a rhythm, from which He composes the beautiful song.

I've also learned that Sabbath needs a system. A plan without a system is just an idea. I bet you've had some ideas that never came to fruition, right? Perhaps, "I'm going to lose weight" or "I want to write a book" or "I'm going to win the lip-syncing world championship." Why didn't it become a reality? Because it was an idea without a system. You might have read the last page or two and thought, *You're right. I should take a Sabbath every week. Not only because God commands it—after all, why is it the only one of the Ten Commandments we think it's okay to break?—but also because I need it. I'm gonna do it!* That's great, but if you don't create a system, those best intentions will likely fade away.

Sabbath is less a command we are bound to keep and more of a promise we're invited into. And because it is an invitation, it's easy *not* to participate. But inside of this invitation is a promise from God that will bring you great blessing and favor in your ReLeading endeavor. I know you'd say you believe every word in the Bible, but do you really believe this promise from God about taking a Sabbath?

> If you watch your step on the Sabbath
> and don't use my holy day for personal advantage,
> If you treat the Sabbath as a day of joy,
> GOD's holy day as a celebration,
> if you honor it by refusing "business as usual,"
> making money, running here and there—
> Then you'll be free to enjoy GOD!
> Oh, I'll make you ride high and soar above it all.
> I'll make you feast on the inheritance of your ancestor Jacob.
> Yes! GOD says so! (Isaiah 58:13–14 MSG).

Your enemy is going to come after the weak spots in your wall, so expect that attack and place guards there. Notice Nehemiah decided to post guards at the weak points *in advance.* He knew it was better to build guard rails at the top of the mountain than to construct a hospital at the bottom of it. What will you put in place before you're so physically tired and mentally exhausted you're not sure you can continue?

4. Expect Distraction

I want you to notice the progression of the enemy's attack strategy. It started with rumors of an intervention (Nehemiah 4:6–8). Then it got more specific with threats of killing and putting an end to the work (4:11–12). Then came the third, and perhaps most insidious attack, which was not to destroy but to distract.

> When word came to Sanballat, Tobiah, Geshem the Arab and the rest of our enemies that I had rebuilt the wall and not a gap was left in it—though up to that time I had not set the doors in the gates—Sanballat and Geshem sent me this message: "Come, let us meet together in one of the villages on the plain of Ono."
>
> But they were scheming to harm me; so I sent messengers to them with this reply: "*I am carrying on a great project and cannot go down. Why should the work stop* while I leave it and go down to you?" Four times they sent me the same message, and each time I gave them the same answer (Nehemiah 6:1–4, italics added).

You've probably heard the saying, *The enemy doesn't need to destroy you; he just needs to distract you.* Although the enemy has many weapons in his arsenal, I believe distraction is his most potent one.

- The enemy used Jezebel to distract Elijah with a death threat after he called down fire on Mount Carmel (1 Kings 18).
- The devil tried to distract Jesus in the wilderness (Matthew 4).
- The Israelites were repeatedly distracted by false gods.
- In his letters, Paul warned the early churches again and again that they were becoming distracted from the pure gospel message.

Why would our story be any different?

In my early days as a pastor, the enemy used a sneak attack to distract me. I was so concerned about our church's survival that I became obsessed with attendance numbers. I was chasing down any rumor of someone who was considering leaving the church.

I was consumed by the fear of losing one more person. To put it another way, I was so focused on the numbers that I forgot what the numbers represented. That's easy to do for many pastors. We become more interested in growing big churches than we are in growing big people. That's a quote I stole from my hero, Pastor Jack Hayford. I had to ask myself, *Why did God call me to ReLead anyway? To ensure Victory Church remained a "megachurch" or to ensure the people of Victory Church remained in Christ?* The enemy didn't have to destroy the church; he just had to distract me from making sure the church was fulfilling its purpose. It took me about a year to realize the enemy's strategy. Then I remembered I was not called to grow a big church; I was called to grow big people.

We need to be ready to defeat distraction.

I'm impressed by Nehemiah's ability to discern what was a distraction and stay focused on his work. He said, "I am carrying on a great project and cannot go down. Why should the work stop while I leave it and go down to you?" What empowered him to ignore the distraction and stay on the wall? I can't help but think it goes back to the moment he responded to the call. "I had not told anyone what my God had put in my heart to do for Jerusalem" (Nehemiah 2:12). If I'm right, we again see the importance of remembering. Nehemiah had not forgotten the *why*. His calling was greater than the chaos and more dire than the distraction.

As you step into your role as a ReLeader, expect distraction.

5. Expect a Miracle

I told you before there were no miracles in this story—except for maybe how quickly they got the work done—but I think I found one. Nehemiah said, "I had not told anyone what my God had put in my heart to do for Jerusalem" (Nehemiah 2:12). Although God did not provide a manifestation of a miracle in the book of Nehemiah, He planted the seed for one to grow in the heart of this ReLeader. The concern for Jerusalem God planted in Nehemiah's heart was paired with the hard work of the people to produce a miracle. Nehemiah didn't wait for a miracle; God used him to *become* the miracle.

As a ReLeader, you do hard things. When we do hard things, God shows up. Sometimes He doesn't do a miracle *for* us; He does one *through* us or *in* us.

When we do hard things, God shows up.

"Sometimes God doesn't do a miracle for us" probably won't be posted on social media or put on a coffee mug. It's not a phrase that prompts shouting or waving of a white hanky in church, but it's important for ReLeaders to understand. Waiting for God to "do a miracle" can keep our hand from the plow. As a ReLeader, you are called to do hard things no one else was willing to do. What should we expect when we're expecting? Perhaps not a miracle. Instead, we expect to do hard things.

Paul was an expert at doing hard things.

> Five times I received from the Jews the forty lashes minus one. Three times I was beaten with rods, once I was pelted with stones, three times I was shipwrecked, I spent a night and a day in the open sea, I have been constantly on the move. I have been in danger from rivers, in danger from bandits, in danger from my fellow Jews, in danger from Gentiles; in danger in the city, in danger in the country, in danger at sea; and in danger from false believers. I have labored and toiled and have often gone without sleep; I have known hunger and thirst and have often gone without food; I have been cold and naked. Besides everything else, I face daily the pressure of my concern for all the churches. Who is weak, and I do not feel weak? Who is led into sin, and I do not inwardly burn?
>
> If I must boast, I will boast of the things that show my weakness (2 Corinthians 11:24–30).

And we thought we had it rough! If you ever need perspective, just read a little about this guy's life, and you'll gain some. Paul experienced every worst-case scenario and just kept working and writing about "rejoicing in the Lord always." It feels like he knew something we don't.

I wonder if we get a glimpse into the mystery that many early church pioneers understood from the apostle Peter:

> **After you have suffered** for a little while, the God of all grace, who called you to His eternal glory in Christ, will Himself **perfect, confirm, strengthen** *and* **establish** you (1 Peter 5:10 NASB1995, bold added).

The Greek word for suffer in this text is *paschō*, which means, 'to experience a sensation or impression of pain.' Peter says that *after* you have experienced a sensation or impression of pain, the God of all grace will do four things:

- Perfect you
- Confirm you
- Strengthen you
- Establish you

ReLeader, your work will be hard, but God promises that He will be with you and that you have nothing to fear. Even more, if you answer the call, He promises to do some things *in* you.

Perfect You

The Greek word here is *katartizō.* It means 'to restore, to prepare, to equip, to fit or to frame.' This is the same word used in Mark 1:19 to describe what James and John were doing to their nets when Jesus saw them. In English it says they were *mending* their nets. They were taking what was broken and putting it back into its original and intended condition.

There is a mending God wants to do in you, and He promises to do it *after* you have suffered. If there's damage that happens as you do hard things, God promises to mend you.

James and John mended the nets to restore them to their best condition, but the real purpose of mending was to prepare the nets to catch something again. It was preparation for their next fishing adventure and the nourishment it would provide.

If there's damage that happens as you do hard things, God promises to mend you.

As you step out and lead, God will perfect you, and part of the purpose is to prepare you for your next mission. What you are currently accomplishing is not just about today; it is simultaneously preparing you for your next season.

Confirm and Strengthen You

Confirm and strengthen share the same root word in Greek, *histēmi.* I did a deep dive into the meaning of this Greek word and discovered it is incredibly rich and takes many English words to describe. Let me share five promises God is saying He will give to you—after you suffer for Him—that all come from this one little word:

1. *To cause to stand, to be placed into position.* God will put you in the positions you need to be in and will give you the strength to stand.
2. *To stand next to.* Not only does God put you into position and stand you up, but He also promises to stand next to you.
3. *To give balance to.* As you experience the turbulence of doing these hard things, God will help you keep your balance.
4. *To make immovable.* When the storms of life come, you will not be moved. He will sustain you and keep you from falling.

5. *To stand unharmed, to be made safe and sound.* God promises protection and safety. This might be God's involvement in the health of your family or with your mental, physical, emotional, and spiritual health.

Wow! If you had all five of those, then you could do hard things, couldn't you? That's why it's so critical that we understand and embrace God's promise. Otherwise, we'll be like most people who think of hard work as an independent endeavor. "Just pull up your bootstraps and do it yourself!" In America we are all about independence. But there isn't much talk in the Bible about us doing life independent from God. In fact, God desires us to be fully dependent on Him. Hard work apart from God's help leads to hard falls. God does call us to do hard things but not to kill ourselves in the process. That is not the heart of a loving Father. He wants to empower you to do what He's called you to do.

Hard work apart from God's help leads to hard falls.

Can I ask what measuring stick you use? I know many people who measure two things: how hard they work and (especially) the results of the work. Many of those people accomplished great things but are now divorced, addicted, or just plain miserable. The proper measuring stick is not *what* you do. The proper measuring stick is *how* you're doing while you do it.

Establish You

'The word translated "establish" is *themelioō*, which means 'to lay the foundation, to found, to make stable, to settle.' When you do hard things, you are laying a foundation for God to build something on top of.

- For Joseph, it was the pit that prepared him for the palace.
- For Moses, it was being evicted from Egypt that prepared him to go back and lead God's people out of Egypt.
- For David, it was being a shepherd in the fields that prepared him for the throne.

In most cases, doing hard things is the prerequisite for big victories.

I love to go to the gym and work out. At the time of me writing this book, my son Jace is 12, and I've started taking him with me as he prepares to start seventh grade football. The other day I was trying to explain to him what happens to our muscles when we work out. I'm no expert, but I told him that when we lift weights heavier than our muscles are used to lifting, our muscle tissues tear. The "pump" you feel is the blood rushing to the trauma to begin the healing process. A quick Google search will tell you this disruption to the muscle cells activates satellite cells from outside the muscle fibers, which rush to the area of damage. These cells replicate, mature into grown cells, and fuse to your muscle fibers. Simply put, your muscles become more resilient and tolerant of lifting heavy weight and capable of lifting more weight in the future. "So," I told Jace, "when I'm doing the hard work of bench pressing 240 pounds, I am doing two things at the same time. I'm accomplishing the current task of lifting the weight *and* simultaneously preparing muscles to lift 245 pounds at a future time."

When I see someone who is stronger than me, I know exactly how it happened. They were willing to lift more weight more frequently. In sports we call that "putting in the work." The same is true in leadership. My friend Sam Chand wrote a book called *Leadership Pain* in which he coined the term "bleedership."[4] He says if you're not bleeding, you're not leading. In fact, he suggests we should never trust a leader who doesn't have a limp. There is something about the hard work of leadership that prepares us for the harder work around the corner.

In every step of my journey, I can see God "establishing" me: first as a vice president at a university, then a campus pastor, then a lead pastor, then a university president. Looking back, I'd now say, *Even when I thought my life was off track, it was never about a track—it was always about a stack.* Like scaffolding stacked over and over to reach new heights, God was always doing a new work *in* me so He could do a new work *through* me. Every step of the way He was perfecting, confirming, strengthening, and establishing me:

- He was perfecting me by mending past pain and working out insecurity, doubt, fear, and anxiety.
- He was confirming me with acceptance as a son and giving me God-given gifts and anointings to fulfill each calling along the way.
- He was strengthening me to lead more people, manage more resources, and do harder things.
- He was establishing firm foundations in me so I could carry more weight and reach new heights.

And He's not done with me yet. He is doing a work in me today that will empower and equip me to do greater things tomorrow.

I've learned we serve a God who does miracles. Not always the one we want and when we want it, but always the one we need. Not always a miracle for us—sometimes a much greater and more necessary miracle *in* us.

From the moment God spoke to me about going out beyond the safety of the shore, I knew I would be in over my head. I think I would have drowned if it weren't for my secret weapon.

Good news: That same secret weapon is available to you. *Read on.*

YOUR SECRET WEAPON

There were a lot of low moments in my ReLeading journeys, but I remember one in particular when it felt like I was experiencing every cliché: I had hit a wall, was at the end of my rope, and hanging by a thread. I didn't know how I could go on or if I wanted to. But I did. I made it.

Do you want to know how?

Yes, you do.

You do because you're going to have some of those awful cliché moments.

When you find yourself there, you need to do what I did, which is what Nehemiah did and what Paul did.

You rely on the secret weapon.

When Nehemiah was filled with an anguished concern about the lack of walls protecting Jerusalem, he had to convince the Israelites to adopt his calling. How did he do it? He told them about his secret weapon.

> Then I said to them, "You see the trouble we are in: Jerusalem lies in ruins, and its gates have been burned with fire. Come, let us rebuild the wall of Jerusalem, and we will no longer be in disgrace." *I also told them about the gracious hand of my God on me* and what the king had said to me.
>
> They replied, "Let us start rebuilding." So they began this good work (Nehemiah 2:17–18, italics added).

Nehemiah tries to get everyone on board by appealing to God's grace, which was on him.

We saw how Paul went through unimaginable hardship. How did he get through it? He had a secret weapon. That's why he could say, "I can do all things through Christ who strengthens me" (Philippians 4:13 NKJV). What was Paul's secret weapon? Grace. "He said to me, 'My grace is sufficient for you, for my power is made perfect in weakness'" (2 Corinthians 12:9).

Grace is also what God promised, through Peter, to those who have suffered:

> After you have suffered for a little while, **the God of all grace**, who called you to His eternal glory in Christ, will Himself perfect, confirm, strengthen *and* establish you (1 Peter 5:10 NASB1995, bold added).

After you have suffered a little while, you will be perfected, confirmed, strengthened, and established. Who is going to do this in you? The God of all *grace.*

Too often we limit our view of God's grace to salvation, but it's so much more. The Greek word is *charis,* which means 'good will, favor, reward, to strengthen, to benefit.'

Grace is our secret weapon.

Grace is our secret weapon.

Hard work *apart* from God's grace produces exhaustion: physical, mental, emotional, and spiritual.

Hard work *with* God's grace produces the fruit of the Spirit: peace, love, joy, patience, kindness, goodness, faithfulness, gentleness, and self-control (Galatians 5:22).

Some people think working hard saps love and joy and patience from your life. No. You can do hard things and still have the fruit of the Spirit.

In fact, earlier I said the proper measuring stick is not *what* you do but *how* you're doing while you do it. So how do you measure how you're doing? The fruit of the Spirit. Jesus said, "Each tree is recognized by its own fruit" (Luke 6:44). We need to ask, *In my ReLeading journey, as I do hard things, what fruit am I producing, not just in my organization but especially in my own life?*

I can work hard *and* rest, push to produce results *and* see fruit in my life, because of my secret weapon—grace.

Let's do a little review of God's plan for ReLeading—of the process He wants to take us through:

REspond: We receive our calling, and we respond.
REmember: We pause and take the time to remember what's gone before us.
REquired: We know we'll be required to do hard things, but we can do them with the empowerment of God's grace.

In the next chapter, we will discover that God doesn't tell us what will be required without also giving us the reassurance of His promises that He will go with us.

4

REassurance

WANTING TO QUIT THE DAY JOB

Have you ever felt like quitting?

Perhaps a better question would be: Have you ever *not* felt like quitting?

I get it.

We're grateful for our calling and find joy in it almost every day. But at the same time, the burdens are heavy, and we are only human.

I recently learned a new word: botheration. It means worries or difficulties. The sample sentence I found is, "He has caused us a great deal of unnecessary botheration."

I didn't know botheration was a word, but just like every ReLeader, I have a long history with it. So here's some of what causes us "a great deal of unnecessary botheration."

LEADERSHIP INSTINCTS: BLESSING OR BURDEN?

If God has gifted you as a leader, then you have a blessing ... *and* burden: You can see the future.

Can you imagine Zerubbabel and Jeshua about to (finally) start their project? If you're a ReLeader, you can. Their minds were racing, always thinking ahead. One hemisphere of their brains devoted to keeping a to-do list and the other devoted to keeping track of obstacles they'd have to overcome. (I am trusting that no neuroscientists will ever read this book.)

You know what I'm talking about because you can see what's coming, and your brain is overworked like an air conditioner in Death Valley in July. It's the gift and burden of having leadership instincts.

- The gift is that you can see into the future of your organization. That makes you aware of the opportunities and potential. That is a tremendous gift you have.
- The burden is that you can see into the future of your organization. That makes you aware of the requirements, challenges, and dangers waiting to ambush you. That is a tremendous burden you bear.

You Can Claw Your Way to the Top, But It's Lonely Up There

We've all heard the saying, "It's lonely at the top." I want to give you a new expression, but first, why is it so lonely for leaders?

It's a strange phenomenon because leaders have teams. After all, if no one's following, then you're not really leading. So how can someone surrounded by people be lonely? In a great blog post, Carey Nieuwhof offers "6 Reasons You Feel Lonely in Leadership,"[1] including what he calls "The Last 10% of Leadership is the Loneliest." He describes how the majority of problems you need to solve as a leader are not solvable by most of the people in your organization. (That's why you get paid the big bucks!) He says that's one of the reasons leaders feel lonely. It's not that you are alone; it's that you are alone with the most difficult decisions in your organization.

So here's my new expression: "It's lonely at the top, but the loneliness for ReLeaders just don't stop." That may not catch on, but I think it's true. If leaders sometimes feel like they are isolated in their offices, then ReLeaders feel like they're abandoned in the middle of the Amazon with no compass.

I'm not suggesting leaders don't have struggles, but there are advantages to building an organization (versus rebuilding). When you are building, there's excitement in the air. It's new! There's innovation! There's anticipation! There's progress! In most settings, the leader is followed and even celebrated as they lead through seasons of launch and growth.

ReLeaders find themselves in a very different environment. They have to run into a firestorm of dysfunction and perhaps trauma. Instead of movement and momentum, there is inactivity and inertia.

This may be a good time to establish the two entry points for ReLeaders and ask you to identify which better describes your situation.

1. **The Restorative Leader.** This is the leader who is brought in to restore and redeem an organization or department.
   These ReLeaders don't just read Nehemiah 4:10—they can *feel* it: "Meanwhile, the people in Judah said, 'The strength of the laborers is giving out, and there is so much rubble that we cannot rebuild the wall.'" The vast majority of ReLeaders are dealt this hand. What they are trying to put back together is so broken it's hard to even know where to start.

2. **The Reinventive Leader.** This is the leader who must follow on the heels of a great leader.

   This is Joshua following Moses in leading the Israelites. It's Gene Bartow following John Wooden as coach of the UCLA Bruins after he won 10 championships, or Tim Cook following leadership legend Steve Jobs, or Andy Wood coming after Rick Warren at Saddleback Church.

   They must establish their own leadership and reinvent how it looks to lead the organization or department without dishonoring their predecessor. While finding their own way, there's always the pressure of measuring up to their predecessor's accomplishments.

Either way, you become the point person for a group of people who are *not* there because they chose to follow you. They are skeptical, at best. But still, you move forward with resolve and determination, regardless of whether a crowd follows.

That is incredibly commendable.

And it can be absolutely lonely.

The worst punishment for a prisoner is solitary confinement. Isolation is about as bad as it gets. But for a ReLeader, it actually does get worse because there are still more causes of botheration. Like comparison.

Crushed by Comparison

They say comparison is the thief of joy. I believe that's true, but I also think comparison can be even more insidious. As a ReLeader, comparison won't just steal your happiness—it will also suffocate your ability to lead as God intends.

I say that from experience. Because as in many ReLeader journeys, there was a lot of "wow!" in the past to be compared to.

At Victory Church, my predecessor was a dynamic leader who had built an incredible church. The church really enjoyed a burst of momentum in the late '90s and early 2000s by putting on large production plays that drew massive crowds. They packed the house for these events and eventually had to move them to the fairgrounds arena to accommodate the growing crowds. The church even launched a dance studio to train those who were in the performing arts. The pastor was an incredibly gifted communicator, hilarious with a mic in his hand, and he could hold thousands of people on the edge of their seats with his well-crafted messages. He could preach a sermon on "Mary Had a Little Lamb," and hundreds would come to the altar to receive Christ. He had a huge vision to "reach a city, change a nation, and touch the world," and he swung hard at any pitch that came down the pipe. Eventually they launched campuses in Las Vegas, Nevada; Corpus Christi, Texas; Norman and Edmond, Oklahoma; and even Maseru, Lesotho, Africa (a small nation near South Africa).

If you're called to ReLead, then you're probably tempted to fall into the comparison trap when it comes to the organization's past or previous leader.

The Former House

If you're a Restorative Leader, brought in to restore and redeem, then it's safe to say that, at some point, the "former house" of your organization was substantial. In other words, what was built in the past was substantial enough that people want to see it rebuilt. When I became the lead pastor of Victory Church, it felt overwhelming to even try to imagine restoring, redeeming, or rebuilding what my predecessor had done.

Does this keep you up at night? Or does it make you dread driving to work in the morning? Does it feel impossible for you to do anything that might live up to the grandeur of what came before you? When you notice someone looking at you in the lobby, do you assume they're thinking, *That poor sap. He believes he can do something special here, but he can't. It's not possible here*?

The Former Leader

When you pioneer a new work, there's no one to compare you to. That's kinda nice. But when you follow someone else, you will be compared to that someone else.

Can you imagine if that someone else is Moses or Elijah? You could make a good argument that they would be on the Mount Rushmore of the greatest people ever to be used by God. Not only did they leave incredible legacies, but Moses and Elijah are also the two people God chose to have a meetup with Jesus on the Mount of Transfiguration.

Moses' résumé is, ahem, not bad. By the power of God, he split a sea down the middle, released the plagues on Egypt, made water pour out of a rock, and called down a miraculous provision of manna and quail from heaven. Oh yeah, in his spare time, he met with God face-to-face and walked away with his face glowing. (No big deal.) When Moses' time on earth was up, the Bible says God personally buried him (Deuteronomy 34:5). I don't know who will do the eulogy at my funeral, but I'm pretty sure it won't be God Himself.

Elijah is one of only a few people with a résumé that stacks up well with Moses'. He told the rain to stop and to start, and it followed his commands. He called down fire from heaven to consume an offering that he had prepared by soaking it first in water. Anything else? Oh yeah, God used him to raise people from the dead, miraculously provide an unending supply of flour and oil for a widow, and he did his own water splitting at the Jordan River. When his time on earth was done, God did not bury Elijah like he did Moses. Instead, God escorted Elijah to heaven in a whirlwind on a chariot of fire driven by heavenly horses.

Can you imagine when the ministry seasons of each of these men came to a close? Duplicating the "glory of the former house" would seem utterly unattainable. How would you like to be the ReLeader following one of these guys? Good luck, Joshua and Elisha!

You and I didn't have to follow Moses or Elijah, but we do know the pressure of following a respected and beloved leader and the temptation it brings to compare ourselves to them and feel like we're less than.

THE GIFT OF REASSURANCE

As a ReLeader, you are surrounded by problems you did not create:

- A financial hole you did not dig.
- An unhealthy staff you did not hire.
- A dysfunctional business model you did not build.
- A toxic culture you did not create.
- A lack of excellence permitted by those who went before and did not have your values.

It can be incredibly discouraging.

When ReLeaders step into their new roles, it's not often met with parades and celebrations. You were brought in because something is broken. When something is broken, people scatter. Those who remain may be suffering with PTSD, cynicism, or a lack of hope.

You were brought in because something is broken.

You walk into all this, and the burden of leadership can feel overwhelming. The potential for failure looms. You may feel isolated, and the loneliness starts to take a toll.

But there's good news.

Great news.

God knows what you're going through. He knows the challenges. He knows how you feel. And He knows what you *need.* Not only does He know but He also offers it to every ReLeader.

Zerubbabel and Jeshua

Lurking in the shadows just beneath the surface of every leader is a fear of failure. In extreme cases, psychologists call it atychiphobia. Fear of failure can paralyze you and keep you from trying something new or taking a risk or moving forward because you're afraid of an unsuccessful outcome. I wonder if these fears are especially pronounced for ReLeaders, who are usually stepping into a situation where there has already been failure and where there is little to no momentum. Our circumstances and our human shortcomings often cast a shadow over our faith in an invincible God.

For Zerubbabel and Jeshua, the fear of failure had to be immense. They were building *the* Temple for *God.* The Temple that came before, that people would surely compare theirs to, was spectacular. They were not sure if they could bring together the resources necessary.

The fear of failure can be debilitating.

I love that we serve a God who is mindful of this. Because He is, He provides a special strength to sustain ReLeaders through their calling. I call this impartation the gift of *reassurance*. We see God, repeatedly, all throughout Scripture, meet every doubt with His assurance. And it's that reassurance that gives the person He's called the boost they need to move forward, even in the face of fear.

We see God give it to Zerubbabel and Jeshua in Haggai 2:9.

> "The glory of this present house will be greater than the glory of the former house," says the LORD Almighty. "And in this place I will grant peace," declares the LORD Almighty.

If I'm Zerubbabel and Jeshua, this is all the reassurance I need. I'm ready to pick up my tools and start rebuilding.

God didn't give them all the answers they wanted. I'm sure He hasn't given you all the answers you're looking for either. God also didn't give them a step-by-step breakdown of how everything was going to come together.

He gave them something better.

He gave them a sneak peek of where they would end up. God's reassurance to them was threefold:

1. *You will finish this work.* That is a Karate Kid crane kick to the fear of failure.
2. *The finished product will be great.* Not only will you finish the work, but it will be great and bring great glory to God.
3. *God will grant peace.* Even amid the chaos of rebuilding what was broken, God will bless you and this place you are building with peace.

Every ReLeader needs reassurance. That's why God gave it to Zerubbabel and Jeshua.

It's also why He gave it to Joshua and Elisha. Remember Moses and Elijah had, at different times, led the Israelites in amazing ways and put together those killer résumés. But, like every leader, they had a last day when their names were taken off the door of the corner office, and a new name was put on. Those new names were Joshua and Elisha. And Joshua and Elisha would *definitely* need God's gift of reassurance.

Joshua

Joshua's installation as Moses' successor was sudden and swift. Just before the Israelites entered the Promised Land, Moses died, and Joshua stepped into his place. What does God do for Joshua? You can guess what He did because of our last chapter—God gave a locker room speech! God started by getting right to the point.

> After the death of Moses the servant of the LORD, the LORD said to Joshua son of Nun, Moses' aide: "Moses my servant is dead. Now then, you and all these people, get ready to cross the Jordan River into the land I am about to give to them—to the Israelites. I will give you every place where you set your foot, as I promised Moses. Your territory will extend from the desert to Lebanon, and from the great river, the Euphrates—all the Hittite country—to the Mediterranean Sea in the west" (Joshua 1:1–4).

Notice at the beginning, Joshua was still referred to as "Moses' aide." That might be your situation. You got bumped up from aide to head honcho. How do you handle that transition?

It happened so quickly for me that it felt like I was thrown onto a roller coaster without warning and no seat belt. A few months after "D-day" (as we called it), our leadership team was at a retreat in California. At this point, no decisions had been made about the future of our church. Quite frankly, I was considering how I could leave the ministry and go back to my previous career in higher education. I was sitting in a hotel room with Michele, and I got a call to come to a room upstairs. I met one of our board members and a few members of our leadership team who asked me if I would consider becoming the interim lead pastor. I was shocked and dazed, but my mouth opened, and I heard myself saying yes. I remember getting on the elevator, going back down to my hotel room, walking in, and asking my wife, "What just happened?" I couldn't believe it. How did I just go from being a campus pastor to the acting lead pastor? How do I handle the upgrade from ministry aide?

God starts His pep talk with Joshua by stating the obvious—"Moses is dead"—but He doesn't spend much time there. Perhaps because God knew dwelling on the past could paralyze Joshua with comparison. Instead, God gives Joshua a vision of the future. He turns Joshua's attention to what is in front of him. God was giving Joshua the very thing every ReLeader needs before they begin their rebuilding journey—reassurance!

After telling Joshua He'd give him "every place you set your foot," God squashes any comparison and doubt that might be loitering in Joshua's mind:

> Your territory will extend from the desert to Lebanon, and from the great river, the Euphrates—all the Hittite country—to the Mediterranean Sea in the west. No one will be able to stand against you all the days of your life. As I was with Moses, so I will be with you; I will never leave you nor forsake you. Be strong and courageous, because you will lead these people to inherit the land I swore to their ancestors to give them (Joshua 1:4–6).

Do you see the same pattern of promises we saw God give in our last chapter? Be strong, I am with you, do not be afraid, and now go. That's the message God gives all His children who are called to do mighty works for His Kingdom.

Imagine sitting in the locker room before going out on the field for your ReLeadership assignment and hearing God say, "No one will be able to stand against you all the days of your life." Is it implausible to think God gives us that same promise today? Were we called by God? Did He spark our enthusiasm for the call? If so, when we respond, why wouldn't we share in that same promise God gave Joshua? Didn't Jesus tell His disciples, "I will never leave you nor forsake you" (Hebrews 13:5 NKJV)? Didn't Paul give us the assurance, "If God *is* for us, who *can be* against us?" (Romans 8:31 NKJV)? If we are confident our assignment was God-given, then we can have confidence the same promise is given to us. Yes, different leader—but same God.

Perhaps the greatest comfort for me comes at the end of verse 5, where God says, "As I was with Moses, so I will be with you." Notice God *didn't* say, "What I did for Moses, I will do for you." He also didn't say, "The miracles I did for Moses, I will do for you." Joshua would need an entirely different set of miracles than Moses had. He wasn't asking for manna and quail, because they now found themselves in the land of milk and honey. He wouldn't require survival miracles in the desert but warrior miracles in the Promised Land. Joshua wasn't desperate for a God who could make water flow from a rock but for a God who could make the sun stand still so they could finish their battle. He didn't need a God who repeated miracles from the past but a God who was with him and could do what was needed *today*.

Sometimes I wonder if we get stuck in the past, asking God to do again what He did before. But as a ReLeader, you don't need God to *do for you* what He did for your predecessor. You just need Him to *be with you* the same way He was with them.

In my new assignment as lead pastor, I did not need a God who could help me launch new campuses—I needed a God who could help me heal the ones we had. I did not need a God who could help me put on massive theatrical productions—I needed Him to help me heal a different kind of drama altogether. I'm so thankful God introduced Himself to Moses as "I Am," because Joshua would need a different "I Am" than Moses. And I needed a different "I Am" than my predecessor. Let's thank God that even when it's a different leader, He's the same God.

Elisha

Like Joshua, Elisha would have to transition from being an aide to his new upgrade. The installation of Elisha happened about as quick as a TikTok video. One minute Elisha is living his life as a farmer, plowing a field with his team of 12 oxen. The next, a stranger throws his cloak around him and in so doing, prophesies Elisha's coming upgrade. The only thing swifter than the calling of Elisha is his response.

> So Elisha left him and went back. He took his yoke of oxen and slaughtered them. He burned the plowing equipment to cook the meat and gave it to the people, and they ate. Then he set out to follow Elijah and became his servant (1 Kings 19:21).

Elisha fully abandons himself and everything else to follow his calling, slaughtering his oxen to remove any temptation he might feel to go back to what once was. His response proved his commitment to his calling.

Like Joshua, Elisha would be following a ministry first-ballot Hall of Fame legend. But Elisha knew that although he would be a different leader than Elijah, he would be serving the same God. We see Elisha's dependence on, even desperation for, God in His last interaction with Elijah.

> When they came to the other side, Elijah said to Elisha, "Tell me what I can do for you before I am taken away."
>
> And Elisha replied, "Please let me inherit a double share of your spirit and become your successor" (2 Kings 2:9 NLT).

Soon Elijah and Elisha found themselves standing at the Jordan River, where Elijah strikes the water, and just like it did for Joshua, it divides. Then Elijah is caught up in a whirlwind as a chariot of fire escorts him to Heaven. Just like that, the aide steps into his upgrade.

Your ReLeader moment will feel similar. One minute you were doing your thing, and the next you're chosen to pick up the mantle of someone who has gone before you. Then you find yourself wondering if you can strike the water and see it part like he did.

Both Joshua and Elisha would stand on the banks of the same Jordan River, wondering if the same God who parted water for their predecessors would part the water for them. Both would realize what every ReLeader learns in their journey: that the *same* God can work through a *different* leader in *different* ways. God gave both Elisha and Joshua that reassurance as they started their ReLeader journeys. They performed different miracles, but it was the same God empowering them.

For Joshua, it was splitting a body of water but a totally different body of water.

Elisha had just seen Elijah part the Jordan River moments earlier. Then we see Elisha experiencing a vulnerable moment of doubt as he watches Elijah taken away in the chariot:

> As they disappeared from sight, Elisha tore his clothes in distress. Elisha picked up Elijah's cloak, which had fallen when he was taken up. Then Elisha returned to the bank of the Jordan River. He struck the water with Elijah's cloak and cried out, "Where is the LORD, the God of Elijah?" Then the river divided, and Elisha went across (2 Kings 2:12–14 NLT).

It seems the same question sprang into Elisha's mind that plagues so many ReLeaders, "Can I do it the way he did it?" And God, reassuring Elisha in his frail moment, gives him the reassurance he needs by allowing Elisha to perform the same miracle.

Some might claim that Elisha doing the same miracle in the same way is a sign that a successor should lead in the same way as their predecessor. You'll hear terminology like, "Does the new leader have the same DNA as the previous leader?" But I believe it's a mistake to assume the ReLeader must be a clone of the previous leader. And I would point out that although Elisha had spent time with Elijah, he was his own man, with his own unique set of gifts and strengths. While it is true that Elisha did the same miracle at the same body of water, he was standing on the opposite side of the river when he did it. Elisha did not need to be the same as Elijah. He could be a completely different leader as long as he was serving the same God.

I encourage you to stop trying to be the same as your predecessor. Don't compare yourself to other leaders. Be the leader God has called you to be. You'll have obstacles in your way, and you'll have to strike the water, but it will probably be from the opposite side of those who have come before you. That's okay, because you're different from them, but you are serving the same God, and you will watch Him part whatever waters stand in your way.

Don't compare yourself to other leaders.
Be the leader God has called you to be.

God wants to give you the gift of His reassurance, and He has several ways He'll hand it to you.

In the Flesh

My caller ID read, "Jimmy Evans." Of course it did. I can't explain how, but he always called at my lowest moments.

One of the ways God has given me reassurance is by sending angels in the flesh. So many people have helped me through my ReLeader journey at Victory Church—people like Jimmy Evans, who became a real pastor to me through that season of my life. Every time I was in a bad place emotionally and my soul was balled up in a fetal position, my phone would ring, and my caller ID said, "Jimmy Evans."

One of those times, Pastor Jimmy said, "Jon, I was on my morning walk along the golf course this morning, and the Holy Spirit prompted me to pray for you, and I have a reassuring word for you."

I believe the words he shared with me were not just for me back in 2014 but are for every ReLeader trying to do something great for God. So this is for *you*.

"Jon," Jimmy said, "You woke up and found yourself standing in a field surrounded by a harvest. This harvest seems to be a crop of nothing but bad fruit. But you are not called to harvest *this* crop, so stop worrying about the fruit surrounding you. The Lord says you are to simply begin focusing on sowing new seed. The fruit won't change overnight. In fact, it will take years. If you focus on the fruit that's in front of you, you will grow discouraged and quit. So take your eyes off that fruit and place your eyes and your faith on the seed that you are sowing."

Wow!

Then he said something that pierced my heart.

"Jon, if you will just keep throwing down seed, one day you'll wake up and be surrounded by the fruit from the seeds you have sown."

He was speaking over me the same thing God spoke over us through the prophet Haggai. Jimmy was challenging me not to focus on the current condition of "the present house," believing that with God's help, "'The glory of this present house will be greater than the glory of the former house,' says the LORD Almighty. 'And in this place I will grant peace,' declares the LORD Almighty" (Haggai 2:9).

Time after time my discouragement was met by the ring of my cell phone and "Jimmy Evans" on my caller ID. One day he called and told me I was in a winter season, but if I looked close enough, I would find that the winter serves a vital purpose. It was such an encouragement I ended up writing a sermon about it: "There Is a WIN in Winter."

In that call, Jimmy explained that winter distinguishes annuals from perennials. Annuals must be replanted every spring, but perennials know how to survive the winter season and come back in the spring all by themselves. It was a light bulb moment. I already knew people are not attracted to broken things. I realized that it's in these winter months of brokenness that you discover who your true warriors are. Those who walk through this season with you are likely called to be generals in your army.

I'm guessing Pastor Jimmy's words apply to and encourage you, but even more I'm wondering if you have a Pastor Jimmy in your life. If so, you know how life-giving it is to receive God's reassurance through a supportive friend. If not, you need one. (Actually, you probably need a few.) Is it possible you are lacking those people in your life because you haven't been vulnerable enough to let anyone know you're struggling? Is there anyone specific God brings to mind when you think about who might be a great, godly encourager for you?

I hope you'll spend some time with that, because we all need to find people to help us live out 1 Thessalonians 5:11: "Therefore encourage one another and build each other up, just as in fact you are doing."

THE SPECIAL SAUCE

ReLeaders need God's reassurance like people need oxygen. Like eggs need bacon. Like bacon needs ... more bacon!

God will deliver His reassurance in all kinds of ways. Sometimes it's through people, and I am so thankful for the people God placed all around me to encourage me and keep me pressing forward. But there's another delivery system God uses to give His reassurance, and it is the special sauce every ReLeader needs.

Where David Got It

The Amalekites raided the camp of King David and his army while they were away and took all the wives and children. Can you imagine King David and his men returning to discover this? They are distraught, and the army turns against David. They're prepared to stone him to death.

What do you do in that situation?

No, I'm serious. What would you do in that situation?

Here's what David did:

> And David was greatly distressed; for the people spake of stoning him, because the soul of all the people was grieved, every man for his sons and for his daughters: but David encouraged himself in the LORD his God (1 Samuel 30:6 KJV).

As a leader, you will find discouragement is the greatest threat to your cause. *Dis* means 'to remove or take out of.' To discourage is 'to remove courage from.' But what we need is encouragement. *En* means 'to place, to attach, or to implant.' Encourage is 'to put courage in.'

Of all the leadership attributes David exemplified throughout his life, I think his ability to encourage himself in the Lord was his superpower. It was the special sauce that empowered David when he needed it most.

Imagine possessing the ability to stay encouraged no matter the circumstance. How amazing would that be?

I want us to think about two difficult moments in David's life when he had the opportunity to practice encouraging himself in the Lord. They're important because we'll face the same challenges as David.

Desire: When Your Timing Is Not God's Timing

It is so tempting to feel discouraged when your desires go unmet. It's especially confusing when you're doing the Lord's work. You feel like you want what God wants, so why isn't He providing?

David had been a shepherd boy, tending the sheep out in the fields. Then one day Samuel shows up and tells Jesse that one of his sons will be the next king. Jesse calls all his sons—*except David*—so Samuel can determine which one is to be anointed. Why not

David? Because he was the youngest, the runt of the litter. Finally, after Samuel rejects all the other sons, Jesse says, "Oh yeah, I forgot, there is one more, the little guy." David is summoned, and Samuel anoints him as the next king of Israel. What does David do next? Multiple-choice quiz:

a. Get fitted with an amazing new robe and crown.
b. Gets honored with a celebratory parade.
c. Goes right back out to the fields where he continued to be a shepherd boy, tending the sheep.

Answer? C. David was anointed as king, and nothing changed.

We don't know David's exact age when he was anointed as king, but we do know he was just a boy. Some Bible scholars believe he waited about 15 years from the time Samuel first anointed him to the day David finally became king of Judah. Then it was another seven years before he ascended to king over all Israel. This means David waited more than 20 years for his destiny to catch up with his desire. That couldn't have been easy for him.

What do you do when you're waiting on God because His timing is not your timing?

You encourage yourself in the Lord.

David prays,

> How long, O Lord? Will you forget me forever?
> How long will you hide your face from me? (Psalm 13:1 ESV).

I love the way he is honest with God, not afraid to pour out his complaint.

And what's the result of David's vulnerable and intimate time with the Lord? He tells God,

> But I trust in your unfailing love.
> I will rejoice because you have rescued me.
> I will sing to the Lord
> because he is good to me (Psalm 13:5–6 NLT).

Long before David became a somebody, God was doing a work in the nobody. David didn't learn to encourage himself in the Lord in the palace; he learned it alone in the fields.

As ReLeaders who are working to rebuild the palace, we need to first learn to encourage ourselves in the Lord alone in the field.

We need to first learn to encourage ourselves in the Lord.

Distress: When Your Way Is Not God's Way

When the Amalekites invaded and took all the wives and children and then the men turned against David, the text says he was *distressed*. Yeah, I imagine so.

When things don't go your way, when they go wrong, you feel distress—*extreme* sorrow or pain. If you're a leader, or especially a ReLeader, you get used to distress like a new parent gets used to diapers.

In fact, David was no stranger to distress even before the invasion of the Amalekites. David's path to becoming king went any and every way but his way. It didn't happen in his timing or in the way he thought it would. He was not ushered to the throne room by a regal processional; he was pursued with spears and swords.

In 1 Samuel 30, we get glimpses into how David encouraged himself.

First, the text says, "But David encouraged himself in the Lord his God" (v. 6). Did you notice the *location* from which the encouragement came? In real estate the saying goes, "Location, location, location." Real estate is all about location, and so is encouragement. David did *not* encourage himself from within himself. He didn't look in the mirror and give himself a pep talk: "I'm good enough, I'm smart enough, and doggone it, people like me." That would have been the wrong location from which to receive encouragement. Location matters. If you tell me you just had the best meal ever, my very next question will be about the location. "Where?" I think some of us struggle because of location. If your location is planted in social media or with negative people, then you'll likely stay distressed. But if your location is *in the Lord* and you are seeking encouragement *in the Lord,* then you will put distress in your review mirror.

Let me give you a practical exercise you can walk yourself through when you feel discouraged or distressed. Since location matters, ask yourself three "where" questions:

1. *Where have my thoughts been?* More times than not, our emotions follow our thoughts. Have your thoughts been in the Lord or in the world?
2. *Where have my eyes and ears been?* Hebrews 12 says that we should "fix our eyes on Jesus" (see v. 2). Romans 10 says that "faith comes by hearing" (v. 17). A quick look at the recent history of where your eyes and ears have been might reveal what led to your emotional state. You might find that screen time and the voices in your ears have had a bigger impact than you thought.
3. *Where have my hands and feet been?* In Acts 20:35, Jesus is quoted as saying, "It is more blessed to give than to receive." Serving others is the quickest way to get your mind off yourself.

We find another indispensable factor for David in the last two words: "David encouraged himself in the Lord *his God.*" There's a possessiveness to that phrase. David didn't just encourage himself in some God he had heard about or been taught of by his parents. God wasn't "The Big Guy" or "The Man Upstairs." He encouraged himself in the Lord *his* God. David had a personal, intimate relationship with God. I think that relationship was forged in the many days and nights he spent alone in the fields, tending the sheep. Day after day he talked with God. Night after night he looked at the stars and let the experience lead him to worship. If we want to move past stress and distress to peace and calm, we need a consistent habit of solitude, so we are truly abiding in Jesus.

I can find reassurance all around me, in all kinds of ways. It can come from a Scripture, a sermon, or a prophetic word. Reassurance comes from spouses, pastors, friends, or mentors. But more than anything else, the secret sauce for your ReLeader journey is to learn to encourage yourself in the Lord. It's been an absolute game-changer for me.

As I've shared, my becoming the lead pastor in 2014 was not met with shouts of rejoicing or celebration. I was coming in on the heels of a moral failure by our founding pastor, attendance was down, giving was down, and we had just lost one of our campuses that had split off in all the chaos. Trust had been lost. Staff morale was desperately low. Making things worse, I was in over my head. I had a grand total of three years of ministry experience and had preached maybe five times in my life. The situation was a mess. I was a mess.

What did I need?

REassurance.

What did God give me?

REassurance.

I would often go back to the worship night when God spoke so clearly to me to leave the safety of the shore and go out into the wind and waves. Even in that terrifying invitation, there was assurance. God had invited me out into the surf with His word that the waves would not destroy me and that the waves would be of grace that would continually wash over me.

Even still, in the first few years of my ReLeader journey at Victory Church, I was really starting to feel the weight of this burden. I liken it to having children. Children are one of the greatest blessings imaginable—and simultaneously the heaviest burden. I've found it's possible for something to be a blessing and a burden at the same time. In fact, I wonder if maybe the greatest blessings come from the heaviest God-given burdens.

During this season, God gave me three prayers that helped me to find strength and reassurance every night before I went to bed. I heard Rick Warren talk about lifting the burdens of ministry in our daily prayer life. I honestly can't remember whether these were his prayers, or he simply inspired me to write them myself. But every night I would pray these three prayers:

1. *"God, this is Your problem, not mine."* I wasn't casting off my calling. I still held on to my responsibility, but I was recalibrating my heart to remember God is the One who called me to this. It was a reminder to me that God loves this church more than I do, and I am simply a vessel He is using. In essence, I was giving God His job back.
2. *"God, if there is someone better fit to lead than me, then I submit my resignation, and I'm willing to do something more difficult."* It wasn't that I didn't like hard work. I would tell God I was willing to do something even more difficult if He called me to it. This was my daily resignation letter to God. I didn't want to hold onto the lead pastor role as something that validated me. This act of submission also served as a daily assurance for me. I knew that I had offered God my resignation and that He had turned it down. That told me I was still the person God wanted in the role and therefore should behave as though God placed me there.
3. *"God, if it is okay with You, I am going to go to sleep now. If You need me, wake me up. Otherwise, I'm going to sleep, and I will wake up tomorrow and pick this mantle back up. I know that while I'm sleeping, You are working things together for my good."* This was a prayer of trust. I knew that there was a lot I didn't know. But I knew Jesus. And the Jesus I knew could be trusted with what I didn't know.

I would lie in bed and pray those three prayers, and every single night I could mentally, emotionally, and physically sense the presence of God come over me and lift the weight off my shoulders. Then I would drift off to sleep. For three years it was a very challenging journey, but for three years I slept like a rock.

I am so grateful for the gift of God's REassurance.

I wrote at the beginning of this chapter, "We're grateful for our calling and find joy in it almost every day. But at the same time the burdens are heavy, and we are only human." While that is true, the special sauce is God's grace and our ability to access it directly from Him. He is the one who touches our lives in a supernatural way and takes us beyond "only human."

5

REfocus

FINALLY

When you are raising kids, there comes that momentous day when the family is *finally* able to go to "real restaurants." In the early years, there is no way the kids could sit quietly for long periods of time. If you tried, then every person in the restaurant would give you judgy eyes while your kid screamed and rolled around on the ground in cracker crumbs like a zoo animal. Sadly, once my kids were old enough to sit still for longer than two minutes, they still didn't quite have sufficient patience for sit-down dining. They just couldn't understand why it was taking so long to cook the food. Finally, it hit me. Every time they had been to a restaurant, it was fast food. I told them, "Guys, this is not Chick-Fil-A. They're actually cooking the food back there. And although it's taking much longer, if we can just be patient, the food is going to be much better for us."

I want to roll my eyes at the childishness of my kids, but then I realize that I can be just like them when it comes to God's plan for my life. Are you like me? We prefer God to serve up something quick. After all, we gave Him our order. He knows what we want, so why can't He produce it *immediately*? When He doesn't, we will sometimes throw spiritual temper tantrums that would impress a toddler. But if we can just be patient, we'll discover God is cooking up something much better for us. And that is especially true in the ReLeader journey, which is a marathon, not a sprint, and thus requires persistent patience until we finally get to, well, *finally*.

We're five chapters in, and we can *finally* start talking about rebuilding.

If you've followed the ReLeader flow of Zerubbabel and Jeshua, then you've had the safety on the starter's pistol for a while. You were called and responded to that spark of enthusiasm. You remembered the past and counted the cost of what would be required for you to forge your way into the future. Now, finally, it's time to click the safety off and fire the gun.

Which is exciting!

And that leads to the inexorable question: *Where do I start?*

Where Do I Start?

July 2, 2018. My first day as president of TKU. I remember it well.

I was still pastoring Victory Church and had accepted this ReLeader role in higher education.

I was sitting in my new office overwhelmed with gratitude. The prospect of this new adventure felt exhilarating. At the same time, I was crippled by the question: *Where do I start?*

You know that feeling. Your calling is exciting and big and broad. Broad is the dilemma. You're called to

- rebuild the culture of the team,
- rebuild financial stability and sustainability,
- rebuild systems that are no longer working, and
- rebuild your reputation in the community.

Where do you start?

I imagine Zerubbabel and Jeshua were presented with the same quandary. God had taken them on quite the journey: calling them, setting their expectations, and giving them the reassurance that He would be with them and that the present house would produce greater glory than the former one. It was time to pick up a hammer and start the work. But after all that buildup, where should they start with the rebuilding? What comes first? There is a clear answer in the book of Ezra.

> When the seventh month came and the Israelites had settled in their towns, the people assembled together as one in Jerusalem. Then Joshua [also known as Jeshua] son of Jozadak and his fellow priests and Zerubbabel son of Shealtiel and his associates began to build the altar of the God of Israel to sacrifice burnt offerings on it, in accordance with what is written in the Law of Moses the man of God. Despite their fear of the peoples around them, *they built the altar on its foundation* and sacrificed burnt offerings on it to the LORD, both the morning and evening sacrifices (Ezra 3:1–3, italics added).

They began with the foundation.

No surprise.

They started by building *the altar* on its foundation.

Wait. What?

What Do You Build Around?

Sure, you start construction with the foundation. I'm no expert, but that seems obvious.

But the altar?

I think most contractors would put the furniture in the building *after* the building is built, not before. Typically, you wouldn't build the building *around* the furniture, but that's exactly what they did.

Why did they do that?

Because the altar was no ordinary piece of furniture. It wasn't a couch, kitchen table, or daybed. (I admit I've never understood why one might need a special bed designed for the day.) They started with building the altar on the foundation because it was at the heart of what the Temple was supposed to be about.

In this biblical narrative about the altar lies a key component of any successful ReLead project. What is at the core of the organization? What should we rebuild everything around?

This is one of many significant differences between the situation facing a leader and the one experienced by a ReLeader. If you are pioneering a new work, then you get the luxury of building however you see fit. But ReLeaders don't get to disrupt the organization's purpose; they have to focus on getting the organization back on its *original* purpose.

ReLeaders focus on the organization's original *purpose.*

THE *WHY*

I have trouble keeping my ...

Oh, sorry, I got distracted.

I sometimes have trouble keeping focus. I've never been tested, but I'm pretty sure I suffer from at least a slight case of attention deficit disorder.

In fact, most of the time I write my sermons (and now the chapters of this book) between 3 am and 7 am. People think I'm crazy, but ... oh, sorry, I was just looking at Instagram for a minute. Where was I? Oh, yeah. People think I'm crazy, but I love that time of day because that is when I can focus. Everyone is asleep, so no one needs me. My phone doesn't ring. Emails don't show up in my inbox. No one is texting. I get more done in these four hours than I can in an entire day. But even in that distraction-free environment, I can still get distracted. I find myself scrolling through social media and thinking, *What are you doing, Jon? How did you get here? Get back to work.*

I have found it's also easy for organizations to lose their focus.

A leader hears directly from God and launches an incredible ministry or business. Founded on that God-given vision and piloted by a healthy leader, the organization thrives. But it turns out success can be dangerous. Why is that so? Distraction. As the organization grows, the leader's influence expands, and their attention can be pulled outside of the mission. Even if a leader stays healthy and engaged, as the organization grows the leader loses the ability to influence every facet of the culture, and mission slip can result.

Some ReLeaders get their opportunities because of a great failure, but others because of success that led their predecessors to lose focus and the organizations to drift.

If you want to know how easy it is to lose your focus in leadership, then just ask these leaders:

- Moses struck the rock when God specifically told him to speak to it. He assumed God would do it the same way as last time. Moses lost his focus.
- Saul started as a humble leader relying on God but ended up consulting a witch, trying to kill the man God chose to be his successor, and offering a sacrifice himself instead of waiting for Samuel to arrive and do it properly.
- Solomon began by seeking God and the wisdom He provided but eventually ended up in forbidden marriages that led him away from his devotion to God.

In Chapter 2, I told you that when a previous leader got distracted it didn't mean he is a bad person. One mistake does not cancel years of faithful ministry. In the army of God, we should not execute our wounded. The ReLeader has a job, and it's not to come in, throw the predecessor under the bus, take the reins of the organization, and create a new *why*. The ReLeader's role is to refocus everyone on the original *why*.

Keep the Main Thing the Main Thing

Simon Sinek authored a powerful book called *Start with Why*.[1] Sinek shows that the most effective and successful leaders start not with what (what we do) or how (how we do it) but with *why*. They organize everything based on, and communicate with their team around, one central compelling *why*. As in, "This is why we do what we do."

Before Jeshua and Zerubbabel scooped a shovel of dirt or moved a single brick from the rubble, they must have asked the question, *Why was this Temple built in the first place?*

God gave the original *why* to King David and King Solomon—they had heard directly from Him. So why would they rebuild with a different *why*?

ReLeaders do their research. They know they are not commissioned to rewrite the *why*, so they make sure they know why God started this organization in the first place.

Part of Victory Church's heritage was being known as a "hospital for the hurting," where all are welcome. Although we have white-collar congregants in our original Warr Acres campus, it is a predominantly a blue-collar church. When I first became lead pastor, a fellow local pastor told me, "You should sell that property and move the church north into the more affluent part of town. You're always going to have financial concerns as long as you're in Warr Acres." Words flew out of my mouth that I probably wouldn't have said if my filter had been functioning properly: "I'm pretty sure if Jesus was in Oklahoma City, He would be in Warr Acres." That was the rude way of saying, "God called Mark and Jennifer Crow to start this church with a core purpose, and that *why* has not changed."

As a ReLeader there are things I *can* change but not the original call. My calling is to refocus our church on it.

Likewise, when I became the president of TKU, I had to ask some questions:

- What is the legacy and God-given core purpose of this organization?
- When God told Pastor Jack Hayford to "found a seminary" at 30,000 feet as he flew home from Promise Keepers on February 16, 1996, what exactly did He speak into Pastor Jack's heart?

As a ReLeader, it's vital to understand the history and original calling God placed on the organization. You are not a builder;

you're a rebuilder. God is not a *redoing* God; He is a *redeeming* God. You bring honor and glory to God when you redeem what was broken. When we were dead in our transgressions, God did not throw us out and start over; no, He redeemed us. Even now, when I make mistakes, slip into sin, or go off the rails, He does not simply pull me out to the dumpster. He restores me so I can become what He's always intended me to be.

ReLeaders do their research. They know why God originally started this organization, and they have no intention of throwing that original purpose out and starting over. At some point before you arrived, someone tried to build the right thing the wrong way. You are now left picking up the pieces. The worst thing you could do is build the wrong thing the right way.

If you have a different purpose or vision for the organization you are stepping into, then you are not a ReLeader, you are an entrepreneurial leader. There's nothing wrong with that; it's just not the right fit for an organization that needs to rebuild. The one you're taking over has a God-given blueprint, and the greatest blessings come with a ReLeader whose main drive is to redeem and restore what God originally established.

If you have been leading an organization for a season, and you just can't seem to get any traction, I wonder if you might be re*doing* instead of re*deeming*.

You are not sent to create the main thing. You are called to keep the main thing the main thing.

On the Threshing Floor

It's time to talk about "its."

Sometimes when I read Christian books, I'm tempted to skim over certain Bible passages because I know I've read them in the past. I hope you didn't do that with that passage in Ezra 3, because there's a nugget in it that's fascinating.

It's the word *its*.

We're told, "They built the altar on its foundation." In the next chapter, I'll tell you how they had to rebuild the foundation of the Temple, but it's fascinating to learn that the altar had its own foundation, separate from the Temple's.

What was the altar's foundation? We find the answer by going back to 2 Samuel 24. Way back before the original Temple was built by Solomon, a plague was coming over the people of Israel, and the Lord commanded King David, "'Go up and build an altar to the LORD on the threshing floor of Araunah the Jebusite.' So David went up, as the LORD had commanded through Gad" (2 Samuel 24:18–19). Threshing floors were always built in high places so the wind could separate the chaff from the grain as it was tossed into the air. This threshing floor of Araunah would become a place of significance for many reasons.

Jewish tradition maintains the altar David built here was on the exact rock Abraham used to assemble his altar in preparation for the sacrifice of Isaac before God intervened.

Even more significant, the threshing floor of Araunah would become the location Solomon chose to build the Temple.

> Then Solomon began to build the temple of the LORD in Jerusalem on Mount Moriah, where the LORD had appeared to his father David. It was on the threshing floor of Araunah the Jebusite, the place provided by David (2 Chronicles 3:1).

There "they built the altar on its foundation." What's the significance for us? As ReLeaders, the core of our organization must be placed back on its original foundation. When we do that, we'll find that foundation is sure, steady, and strong and can withstand any moral failure, financial corruption, scandal, fall, or mission drift. As you start your ReLeader endeavor, place the core of the organization back on this foundation.

> So this is what the Sovereign LORD says:
>
> "See, I lay a stone in Zion, a tested stone,
> a precious cornerstone for a sure foundation;

the one who relies on it
will never be stricken with panic" (Isaiah 28:16).

You may not be ReLeading an organization that was founded on Christian values, but if you are, this verse speaks of the one foundation that cannot be destroyed. It's the one thing you can center everything on, feeling confident it will hold any weight you place on it. It is the sure foundation of Christ our cornerstone. If you lead a Christ-centered organization, He is the foundation your *why* rests upon. And that's why, as a ReLeader, you don't get the luxury of changing the *why* of your organization. You can change the *what* and the *how*, but you must leave the *why* intact.

If you lead a Christ-centered organization, He is the foundation your why *rests upon.*

DESPITE THE FEAR

When I first became lead pastor in the fall of 2014, I knew there would be some *whats* and *hows* that needed to be changed. One of those challenges was a dance studio. In the early days of Victory Church, Easter productions and other theatrical events were a part of their *how*. Because of this, the church launched a dance school. The director was an amazing man who had stewarded it well for many years and had done nothing wrong. However, the church had stopped doing productions and theatrical plays years before, but the dance studio still remained. A large portion of the clientele did not attend our church, and the financial balance sheet for this business did not balance. The church's *why* no longer required this *what*. It was something I had to sunset, but I was early on in my leadership role and knew the backlash would be great. And it was. When we made the announcement, it caused massive ripples.

There comes a time in every ReLeader's journey when they fear the response of the people. That's where I was, but despite my fear, I knew it was the right thing to do for the organization.

There's an interesting phrase in the text in Ezra that spotlights this fear every ReLeader faces in refocusing the organization on its *why*.

> *Despite their fear of the peoples around them*, they built the altar on its foundation and sacrificed burnt offerings on it to the LORD, both the morning and evening sacrifices (Ezra 3:3, italics added).

Now in this particular text, it seems as though the "people around them" is referring to those living in the area, not necessarily the workers that are rebuilding the Temple. But one thing is clear: fear was present. There was something about "those people" that caused the Temple rebuilders to fear the ramifications of restoring the altar. Fear that had to be overcome. In the heart of every ReLeader is a "fear of the peoples around them."

We see it throughout the Bible:

- Aaron's fear of the people caused him to melt down jewelry and cast a golden calf.
- King Saul's fear of the people caused him to sin against God.
- Peter feared being associated with Jesus and so denied Him.

Some of the biggest mistakes leaders make are due to their fear of people.

The fear in Zerubbabel and Jeshua was palpable enough that it led Ezra to put it on paper, so we have it documented for us thousands of years later. But what were they worried about? After all, why wouldn't the people want to rebuild the altar? Remember that 70 years prior, King Nebuchadnezzar invaded Jerusalem, destroyed the Temple, and removed almost all the Jewish people from their homeland. But there was a remnant left in Jerusalem:

"The commander left behind some of the poorest people of the land to work the vineyards and fields" (2 Kings 25:12).

The remnant who remained in Jerusalem would have tried to stay faithful to God and put the sacred back in place. These people were not priests. They were not anointed to do the work. Most theologians and Bible scholars believe they likely put up a rudimentary, makeshift altar at the original location. If so, before Zerubbabel and Jeshua could rebuild the altar, they first had to tear down the crude altar the people had used for years. The thought of asking the people to do that brought great fear to the ReLeaders.

This offers a great word of warning to every ReLeader. There will be people in your organization who resist your leadership or change. Part of what leads to this is an unhealthy silo culture. Patrick Lencioni wrote a fantastic book on the topic that you should add to your reading list: *Silos, Politics, and Turf Wars.*[2] Organizations without great leadership create cultures of silos and turf wars. Instead of everyone working together for a common purpose, team members abandon teamwork and go into self-preservation (or self-promotion) mode. Playing on the text we're studying, it's like they build their own altars (or idols) that become their sacred cows. And they will view as an enemy anyone who comes along and challenges or disrupts the system or structure they've put in place.

Help, I'm a People Pleaser

Several years ago, the Holy Spirit did a real work in my heart. As He revealed my orphan heart (see Chapter 1), He convicted me that fear was driving me. In many cases, this fear manifested itself through my desire to please people. Ouch! That was not a fun thing to hear from the Holy Spirit. But it was critically important in making me a better ReLeader. I ended up studying this issue in depth and later writing a sermon called "Help, I'm a People Pleaser."

I love that the verse says, "*Despite their fear of the peoples around them*, they rebuilt the altar on its foundation." Their first temptation was to buckle because of the people's desires. Fear is always a lie about tomorrow whispered to you today. ReLeading takes guts. Typically, when you come into the organization, you are viewed not as the hero but as a threat. In the eyes of many, you are on probation. You are guilty until proven innocent. It's a tricky balancing act because you must win over the trust of the people without catering to their every demand or pretense. People pleasers will have a very difficult time making progress as a ReLeader.

Here are five questions you should answer honestly to reveal if you have people pleaser tendencies.

1. *Are you preoccupied with what other people might think?*
   Of course, we should always consider the impact our decisions will make on others, but we shouldn't be paralyzed by their opinions of us.

2. *Do you have a hard time saying no?*
   You can be doing a lot of things but also doing a lot of wrong things. Not that you're doing bad things, but you might be doing what's good instead of what's great, what's urgent instead of what's important, or what's essential to a person rather than to God. Are you saying yes because it's important to the mission or because you're afraid of disappointing people and desperately want them to like you?

3. *Do you complain about being too busy?*
   You might be too busy because you spend so much time meeting everyone's demands. I know I've struggled with this. When every staff member, client, or congregant wants to do lunch with you, how do you meet everyone's expectations? There are only so many lunches! I mean, I'm a fan of "second lunch," but c'mon. If your calendar is overflowing, then it may be a sign that you're a people pleaser who struggles to say no.

4. *Are you sometimes quick to say you agree, even when you don't agree?*
   Have you been there? Someone is presenting an idea or a plan, and deep down you know it's not the right direction. You should say no, but you hear a voice telling you, "That just might work" and realize it's your voice. That probably reveals people pleaser tendencies in you.
5. *Do you often avoid conflict and difficult decisions?*
   No one likes conflict, but ReLeaders must become conflict seekers. It's like someone who has cancer. You don't kill cancer by avoiding it. You have to fight the cancer cells. And conflict is the only path to a healthy culture. ReLeaders seek conflict and resolve it in a healthy manner. If there is cancer in your organization, you don't ignore it or transplant it to another part of the body. Instead, you eradicate it. But people pleasers bristle at that.

How do we find the balance? How do we gain people's trust and love them with the love of Christ while refusing to tolerate unacceptable behavior? As usual, Jesus models this response so well for us.

> Now when He was in Jerusalem at the Passover, during the feast, many believed in His name as they observed His signs which He was doing. But Jesus, on His part, *was not entrusting Himself to them,* because He knew all people, and because He did not need anyone to testify about mankind, for He Himself knew what was in mankind (John 2:23–25 NASB, italics added).

Jesus' ministry caused many to believe but led others to reject and eventually kill Him. In the midst of this we see, "But Jesus, on His part, was not entrusting Himself to them." Wow!

Here are three quick lessons we should learn from Jesus on how to not be a people pleaser:

Know Your Role

In team sports, the only path to victory is if every person knows their role. The linemen in football know their role is to block for the quarterback or running back. The pitcher in baseball or soft-ball knows their role is to deliver the pitch, not run to the outfield and catch the fly ball. Jesus knew His role, and it was not to please people. A downfall for many leaders is not fully understanding (or embracing) their role. When you know and are focused on your purpose, it will drive your priorities. But if you're a people pleaser, then *people* will drive your priorities.

Know Whom to Fear

The text in John 2 says that Jesus "was not entrusting Himself to them." The Greek word for entrusting is *pisteuō*, which means 'to credit, to place confidence in.' When we live to please others, we entrust ourselves to those people, so we misplace our confidence. When we misplace our confidence, we misplace our fear. As God warns us in Proverbs,

> The fear of man brings a snare,
> But whoever trusts in and puts his confidence in the Lord will be exalted and safe (Proverbs 29:25 AMP).

When we are tempted to wonder what people are going to think, we should ask ourselves, *What am I afraid of?*

When I first became a lead pastor, it was on the heels of a moral failure, and people were headed for the exits. I realized everyone loves to see a good wreck at a stock car race, but once the car is taken off the track, few stick around to watch it get rebuilt. For about two years, I was terrified of people leaving the church. I let it control me. I spent far too much time trying to convince people not to leave. I was catering to their demands, answering email complaints, and going to lunches and coffees until I was blue in the face (and full in the stomach). I now realize I was fearing the wrong thing. I should have concerned myself not with the size of the church but with the size of my people. I was not called to grow a big church—I was called to grow big people and let God determine the size of my church.

I realized I had the wrong motivation. But I was encouraged to realize I was in good company, as many of God's children struggled with misplaced fear:

- Abraham feared man, so he lied and said Sarah was his sister.
- Moses feared whether the Israelites would accept him as their deliverer.
- King Saul feared man. "Then Saul said to Samuel, 'I have sinned. I violated the LORD's command and your instructions. *I was afraid of the men and so I gave in to them*'" (1 Samuel 15:24, italics added).
- Peter was so concerned about being accepted by man that he denied his Messiah three times.

The only healthy fear is fear of the Lord. "The fear of the LORD is the beginning of wisdom" (Proverbs 9:10). If you want to ReLead to your fullest potential, know whom to fear.

The only healthy fear is fear of the Lord.

Know Which Witness Matters

I was in seventh grade basketball, and we were doing typical fundamentals drills at practice. Being in seventh grade, we were new to our ever-changing, testosterone-filled bodies. Suddenly, in walked the junior high cheerleading team. Every boy immediately changed their game. We were all showing off, trying to make the furthest shot possible, jumping up and showing we could touch the bottom of the net. The coach immediately shut down practice, called us over, and said, "There is only one person in this gym that you need to impress, and that's me. If you want to play in the game, impressing those cheerleaders won't get you off the bench. Play to the coach, not the fans."

Honestly, who are we trying to impress? This has become a real problem in ministry. So many today measure successes by the size of the organization, budget, influence, and attendance. But John 2:25 says Jesus "*did not need anyone to testify* about mankind, for He Himself knew what was in mankind." I love that He didn't need anyone to testify. This word testify in Greek is *martyreō*, and it means to utter honorable testimony, give a good report.' Shouldn't leaders ask themselves, *Who do I need to testify for me? Who is it that I'm trying to prove myself to? Am I playing for the fans or for the coach?*

Paul understood this temptation, and he disciplined himself to fight against it. He wrote, "On the contrary, we speak as those approved by God to be entrusted with the gospel. *We are not trying to please people but God,* who tests our hearts" (1 Thessalonians 2:4, italics added). He emphasized this again when he wrote, "Obviously, I'm not trying to win the approval of people, but of God. If pleasing people were my goal, I would not be Christ's servant" (Galatians 1:10 NLT).

Before you can rebuild the central purpose of your organization, you first have to tear down the attempts of others to define what is central. If you're a people pleaser, then you'll be held back by fear because for ReLeaders, pleasing God often means disappointing people.

CORE VALUES

Why did your organization fall apart? Perhaps because it lost its focus. To rebuild, it's imperative to give the organization focus—not a new focus but the one that was its original foundation.

It's the same *why*, but you'll probably need to articulate it in a different way.

We're about to see the Israelites rebuild the foundation of the Temple. It was the same foundation at the same location, but I bet it wasn't precisely the same. And then we'll watch as they rebuild the Temple. The purpose of the Temple—to gather for worship, to offer sacrifices, to experience the presence of God—was the same, but it didn't look exactly the same.

As ReLeaders, we give our organization back its *why,* and we work to make sure it truly becomes the focus and driving force. To do that, we come up with and communicate clear, compelling core values.

As ReLeaders, we give our organization back its why.

CREATING YOUR CORE VALUES

The process of creating core values looks slightly different from organization to organization. There are countless variables in your culture that could affect the way you walk this out, but there are some important things I learned through the process of ReLeading that should help you in your journey.

The Purpose

My wife and I battle over the coffee we will drink each morning. I prefer a strong, dark roast, whereas she prefers what I would call a "fufu" vanilla bean or hazelnut flavored coffee.

Who wins?

She always does, of course.

But regardless of who wins, we must use a filtration system in which the chosen flavor of coffee is fused into the water. Doing that ensures that what goes through the filtration system comes out with the same right taste.

Our organizations are no different. And core values are the filtration system that ensures you create a consistent culture and product.

One of your very first tasks as a ReLeader is to establish your core values. While mission statements are important, and you should create one, I've found core values have far more impact. A mission statement without core values is like having an engine with no gasoline.

Why are core values so essential? I would argue values create culture, and culture creates momentum. Peter Drucker famously coined the phrase, "Culture eats strategy for breakfast." Values, when established and communicated with clarity and regularity, create a shared language that the entire community begins to emulate. Culture may eat strategy for breakfast, but if you don't have clear core values, your culture will eat you for lunch. If you want to change the way your community behaves, start by changing the way they talk. I love what we're told about the power of words in Proverbs, "Your words are so powerful that they will kill or give life" (Proverbs 18:21 TPT). The same is true of the culture of your organization. One of the most important steps in any ReLeader's success is changing the way people in the organization talk.

The Priority

When we focus on core values first, we are building the spiritual before the physical; the *why* before the *what*; the altar before the walls. If you are stepping forward to ReLead, I cannot emphasize enough how vital this is. No matter what type of organization you are ReLeading, the most impactful change happens from the inside out, *not* the outside in. Fortunately, we have an incredible guide. The Bible is full of promises to those who see them, get in alignment with them, and then experience the fullness of them in their lives. It is no different in leadership. If you are called to lead, then you must ask yourself the question, *Where am I leading these people?* This forces the leader to ask some questions about motives that rest deep in the secret places of our souls:

- Are we looking to be famous?
- Do we care mostly about success?
- Is it really about financial increase?

Perhaps God's greatest blessings come to those whose true motives line up with their core values? If you want to make sure everyone is tasting the same coffee in your organization, then you might want to make sure God likes the taste of it first.

The Pace

When you first arrive, you'll be tempted to start replacing people, policies, and processes. After all, you're a sharp leader, and the changes required are obvious to you. Can I encourage you to *not* make those moves too quickly? Turning this ship around will take time. And a ship that turns too quickly risks losing its cargo, crew, and the community on board.

In one of my many impatient leadership moments, I talked to Pastor Brady Boyd. I asked him how long it took him to change the culture of New Life Church, where he was ReLeading. He said, "Jon, it took me five years to change the culture here, and you can expect it to be about the same for you." Can you say, "punch in the gut"? It was not the answer I wanted, but it was the best thing I could have heard in that moment. It was an epiphany: This would be a marathon, not a sprint. That realization removed some of the pressure I felt to "make this happen" quickly. It *would* happen, but *one at a time:*

- One decision at a time
- One move at a time
- One prayer at a time
- One policy at a time
- One sermon at a time
- One meeting at a time

That's what I started doing, and over time, the ship started turning. And I was determined to stay there to ensure it made the entire turn. That's the role of a ReLeader.

The Process

How do you come up with these values? Do you lock yourself in a secluded cabin with a vat of coffee, a case of Diet Coke, and a couple of cans of baked beans, vowing not to come out until you've written the core values?

Nope.

You may have a good feel for what the core values need to be, but the role of a leader is to make sure the community goes on the journey with you.

The worst thing a ReLeader can do is create the core values alone, plaster them all over the walls, and present them like the new Ten Commandments. While these values need to come from your heart and the vision God is giving you, you must invite others into the journey of crafting and articulating them.

Good ReLeaders invite others on the journey to articulate the vision and values. A *great* ReLeader is able to take what God has placed in their heart and, with great skill, help everyone to own the ideas like they were the ones who created them. ReLeaders have no insecurity that demands they get the credit and the glory. They're comfortable enough in their own skin to have the vision in their mind, and then watch others "discover" what they knew all along.

Good ReLeaders invite others on the journey to articulate the vision and values.

Writing Your Core Values

At some point, preferably sooner rather than later, you need to write your core values so they're on paper and can be shared, read, and start to bleed into the life of your organization.

While you're walking through this step in your ReLeader journey, I would highly recommend the book *Made to Stick* by Chip and Dan Heath.[3] They explain that the difference between ideas that are remembered and take hold versus those that die and are forgotten is the leader's ability to make them "sticky."

Here are four quick thoughts on how to make your core values sticky:

1. Keep them few.

I would suggest seven or eight core values at most. You want people on your team to know these values so that they act as a guide and a filter in decision-making. Will people remember 12 core values? I doubt it. Can they remember seven? Maybe. With core values, less is more.

2. Keep them short.

Do you know the acronym KISS—Keep It Simple, Stupid? Again, we don't want the core values to just be a poster on a wall. We want people to remember the core values. The issue is that we all have a lot to remember: birthdays, anniversaries, work calendars, home calendars, kids' sports calendars, school calendars, changing our fantasy football starting lineup. Most people are just trying to remember to eat lunch every day because their schedule is so packed.

Let's say you wisely keep your core values narrowed down to seven, but each one reads like the Gettysburg Address (which was a relatively short speech but is a beast to memorize). If you do that, then I doubt your team will remember them. I'd encourage you to consider making each of your core values just a word or a phrase.

3. Keep them achievable.

People like to win. Success tends to improve morale and increase enthusiasm.

If you make your core values something like

- change the world,
- reach the globe for Jesus,
- end world hunger, and
- put a smile on every baby's little face

then they could be *de*motivating—because they all feel unachievable.

Instead, write core values that people can live out and accomplish every day they come to work.

Here are a few examples:

- We give up things we love for things we love even more. —Life.Church
- We are Kingdom-minded first.—Victory Church
- Own the outcome, whether it's good or bad.—Dunkin' Donuts
- We steward God's resources well and with radical generosity.—Victory Church
- Accountability: If it is to be, it's up to me.—Coca Cola
- We are faith-filled, big-thinking, bet-the-farm risk takers.—Life.Church

When a core value is read, everyone in the organization should be able to say, "Yep, that's what we do." They must be action-oriented statements that inspire others to think, *I want to be a part of that!*

4. Keep them on repeat.

The biggest mistake I see organizations make is to create values, put them on their website and their walls, and then never talk about them.

To make them stick, to get them to *actually* be your values (not just aspirations), you need to talk about them and then talk about them more. Then find a different way to talk about them.

It's been said that it's not until you get sick and tired of talking about your values (or mission or vision) that others are just starting to really hear them and care about them.

The work of writing your core values happens mostly behind the scenes, but it may be the most important thing you do in the early days of your ReLeader journey. It cannot be skipped, rushed, or delegated.

This work will refocus your organization and will be what lives on from your leadership after you're gone.

When you construct a building, the height will depend on the strength and depth of the foundation. Establishing core values that call your organization back to its original *why* in a compelling and actionable way is the beginning of the process that creates a foundation you can build on. As the core values catch on and people begin to live them out, you will get a team moving together in the same direction. You'll find your organization has the strength to bear weight, and growth will start to become a real possibility again.

Creating Core Value Momentum

I've given you some tips on how to come up with sticky core values, and encouraged you to communicate them consistently, but what's the process that gets you there? I would suggest two key components.

1. Meet with Your Core

Start by meeting with your leadership team. This team will look different depending on the type and size of your organization. It's possible you may even come into a situation where there is no leadership team. If so, I would find some way to establish one.

Once you've established this team, you need to retreat with them. This should be a smaller group of probably no more than three to five people. I know Jesus had 12 disciples, but He also had a smaller group of three (Peter, James, and John).

In my situation, I took this group on a three-day retreat to an offsite location. We felt that getting away was helpful to create an environment without distraction and in which we could bond at a deeper level.

As you start your retreat, you can share some of your thoughts and give some direction but not too much. You may not realize it yet, but your voice is the loudest. If you share too much, too soon, then you will extinguish the creative energy of your team, which wars against your goal for these meetings. You want to cultivate discussion. Andy Stanley said it best: "Leaders who refuse to listen will eventually be surrounded by people who have nothing to say."

I started by standing in front of a massive whiteboard and asking my team to give me words that describe the type of culture we wanted our organization to bleed. Not sentences, not even phrases, just words. If you do this, you might receive words like healthy, generous, servant, unity, accountable, honest, loyal, empowered, equipped, powerful, or transformed. There are no wrong answers in this stage.

In the next phase, you'll challenge your team to narrow the field. Let's imagine they came up with 85 words. You might ask them to narrow the list down to 20. This will begin to develop thoughtful and intentional conversation. Then, after a coffee or snack break, you'll smile and tell your team, "Now we need to get our list to seven. What are the seven words that best describe uniquely who we are and who we want to be?"

After you narrow the list to seven, work with your team to take those words and articulate sentences or, better yet, phrases that describe the values that will define and transform your culture.

If you show them the general target and you have the right team in place, chances are they will find the same bullseye you envisioned before this group met.

You will also discover aspects of where God wants to take your church that you did not see. God will gather a team around you that can help you see what you'd never see on your own.

2. Meet with Your Bell Cows

You now have your leadership team on board. You feel like everything is ready to go and you can hit the print shops and get the new core values on some posters with a nice-looking font.

But no. Not just yet.

First, you need to get buy-in. But how can you get buy-in from every single constituent in your organization?

Four months into my ReLeader assignment at Victory Church, our leadership team had met, and we were about to change the vision statement and core values of a 20-year-old church. It was a massive change and very early in my leadership tenure. I knew introducing this shift too quickly could be leadership suicide. I needed buy-in, but how could I get it when we had around 50 on staff and thousands of congregants? I could never sit down with every one of them.

I realized if I really wanted the new values to stick, I had to meet with the bell cows. There's an old leadership analogy called "bell cow leaders." On many cow farms in the past, you might have seen one cow in the herd that had a bell hanging around its neck. The purpose of the bell was not for the cow; it was for the farmer. The farmer would identify the cow that all the other cows seemed to follow and place a bell around its neck. The farmer knew he could never go out and individually get each cow to come back to the farm for dinner, but if he could get the bell cow to come, then all the others would follow.

Your organization has bell cows—people whom others listen to and follow. Being a bell cow has nothing to do with a title and everything to do with influence. These are the people you meet with next. If you don't get them on board, you could lose a substantial amount of momentum and may spend the next two years either trying to rebuild trust or replace people you've lost.

Your meetings with the bell cows will be similar to the meetings with your leadership team, but you want to give them a little more guidance. You might take them through the same process with the whiteboard. As the focus narrows, an astute leader can give prompts and cues that can help shape a similar outcome. I don't see this as manipulation. Your goal here is not to redo the process but to help them come to similar conclusions and start to own a shared, God-given vision for the organization. Again, the best leaders are the ones who, while knowing and developing the entire vision for the future, have everyone else convinced it was their idea.

Make sure they know their voice at the table is important, but their voice as they leave the table is *vital.*

You want to give them a voice at the table. This is not just a "rubber stamp" group. In fact, when I went through this process at TKU, it was this group of bell cows that took the seven or eight values our lead team came up with and helped us carve them down to what we would brand as our "Core 4." They even developed icons to go with each core value. It was this group that made our values "sticky" and ready for prime time.

As this meeting concludes, take time to acknowledge how important their influence is and how grateful you are for their important work in the organization. Encourage them to live out these values as their own and help champion the cause. If you get this group on board, then more than likely the whole herd will follow.

It's time to rebuild, so where do you start?

Zerubbabel and Jeshua began by rebuilding the altar. Why? Because that was their *why,* and you must start with the *why.*

As ReLeaders we want to refocus our people around our common cause, and I've found the best way to do that is through coming up with and communicating clear, compelling values.

What's next?

Now it's time to rebuild the foundation.

6

REestablish

GO DOWN BEFORE YOU CAN GO UP

For about a month after the announcement was made that trust had been lost and the founding pastor was gone, our church was *packed*. It turns out a lot of people come and stand in the front yard to watch a house burn to the ground, but very few stick around to watch it get rebuilt. For about a year, we tried everything to recover. We would try gimmicky sermon series, events, guest speakers, anything to get people back in the seats. While none of those things are necessarily wrong, it quickly became apparent that we were going to have to dig a little deeper down before we could go up.

In fact, before we could build anything back, we first needed to form a foundation.

And that brings us back to our story.

> In the second month of the second year after their arrival at the house of God in Jerusalem, Zerubbabel son of Shealtiel, Joshua son of Jozadak and the rest of the people (the priests and the Levites and all who had returned from the captivity to Jerusalem) began the work (Ezra 3:8).

Do you see that? They "began the work."

We learn from Zerubbabel and Jeshua that before you can build high, you have to dig deep. Just a few short verses later, we see what beginning the work accomplished.

> When the builders laid the foundation of the temple of the LORD, the priests in their vestments and with trumpets, and the Levites (the sons of Asaph) with cymbals, took their places to praise the LORD, as

> prescribed by David king of Israel. With praise and thanksgiving they sang to the LORD:
>
> "He is good;
> his love toward Israel endures forever."
>
> And all the people gave a great shout of praise to the LORD, because the foundation of the house of the LORD was laid (vv. 10–11).

Before they ever went up with the structure, they went down with a foundation. It was such a vital part of the process, when they were finished with the foundation, they stopped and celebrated as if the Temple was completed. That's how important God sees this step in your ReLeader journey.

In October 2012, Oklahoma City welcomed its newest skyscraper to the skyline. Standing 844 feet tall, it was the tallest building in the state of Oklahoma. Construction began in 2009. My neighbor at the time was the man brought in to build the most important part of the project. He relocated his family from Atlanta so he could oversee the construction of the foundation. He lived in Oklahoma and worked on the foundation for more than two years. One day I asked him, "How does it feel to dedicate your life to something no one will ever see? I mean, people will drive by this building for decades and be in awe of the height and beauty of the structure, but no one will ever say, 'Wow, would you look at that foundation?'"

His reply to my question was swift and incredibly insightful. Without hesitation, he simply said, "The height of the structure is fully dependent upon the depth and quality of the foundation. Without me, there is no structure. It might not be the most easily noticed element of the build, but it is the most important."

What an amazing picture of how it looks like to be a ReLeader. What if our name is never in lights? What if we never see the structure fully built, but our purpose is to build the foundation for future generations?

The world may not pay as much attention, but that is a high calling.

In fact, laying the foundation was God's calling on Abraham's life. He was given a covenant with God that was all about the future—he would be the "father of many nations." Hebrews 11:9–10 says,

> By faith he made his home in the promised land like a stranger in a foreign country; he lived in tents, as did Isaac and Jacob, who were heirs with him of the same promise. For he was looking forward to the city with foundations, whose architect and builder is God.

We see that same focus on the foundation when Solomon built the original Temple. God had told Solomon, "I will give you a wise and discerning heart, so that there will never have been anyone like you, nor will there ever be" (1 Kings 3:12). As Solomon built the Temple, he began with more wisdom than anyone—*ever.* Equipped with all that wisdom, Solomon invested his time and resources in the Temple's foundation.

> Solomon had seventy thousand carriers and eighty thousand stonecutters in the hills, as well as thirty-three hundred foremen who supervised the project and directed the workers. At the king's command they removed from the quarry large blocks of high-grade stone to provide a foundation of dressed stone for the temple (1 Kings 5:15–17).

I think it's safe to say Solomon understood the importance of a strong foundation.

Caused Collapse

The headline read, "Poor foundation caused collapse that left 11 dead."[1] It happened in India in December 2016, and the government had civil engineers determine the cause of the collapse. What was it? "Excessive load on the foundation." It turns out the builders constructed a six-story building on a foundation that was only designed to handle a four-story building, and many other aspects of the foundation construction were deficient.

As a ReLeader, your first instinct is immediately to do whatever you can to cause growth. You know it's going to take considerable time to bring the size of your church or the revenue of your business back to where it was before and move beyond, so you want to get started.

I get it. That makes sense. But there is essential foundation work you must do first. And if you neglect it, then any growth you achieve will be an excessive load on the foundation and likely cause collapse.

Solomon's Temple construction began with laying a massive foundation. And Zerubbabel and Jeshua started the *re*building of the Temple by *re*constructing the foundation.

We could get lost in the beauty of the symbolism of what happened in the Bible and how it compares to those of us who are in rebuilding efforts today, but I think it would be more beneficial for us to get practical.

What exactly is the foundational work for us?

We've already established the core values. We've refocused our team on our *why* and committed to rebuilding on the foundation that needs no repair—Jesus Christ. It's about time to start building and to finally see growth happen. But what needs to be in place before that?

Let's look at three main things we need to build to repair the foundation of our organization:

1. Trust.
2. People.
3. Systems.

BUILD TRUST

What do you say to your congregation after you've just been named lead pastor following a massive church meltdown caused by the founding pastor's moral failure?

That is exactly the question I was asking the first time I went on stage in my new position at Victory Church. I didn't realize it at the time, but the Holy Spirit gave me a word that I believe was the single most important thing I said to the congregation. It was a request: "I am asking that you credit me trust."

I took them to Genesis 15 where God credited Abraham with righteousness. Abraham had done nothing to earn it or prove he was worthy of it. God simply accounted it to him, freely and in advance.

My word to the church went something like this:

> I know trust has been lost and the bucket has been emptied, but I'm asking you to credit me trust. Many of you do not know me. I've done nothing to earn your trust, and I haven't proven to you that I'm even worthy of it. But if you will credit me some trust today, I will work hard to pay it back to you year after year as long as I get to be your pastor.

To set a foundation on which you can grow, you must first learn the complicated and slow process of building trust. Stephen Covey says, "Trust is the glue of life. It's the most essential ingredient in effective communication. It's the foundational principle that holds all relationships."[2]

The difficulty in receiving trust is that many ReLeaders come into their positions because trust has been lost.

That was the case in my situation at Victory Church. A great man who had built a great ministry made one massive mistake, and the principle of trust evaporated from the church. It has been said, "Trust is gained by the spoonful and lost by the bucketful," and we experienced that proverb firsthand. I wonder if that's even more true in a church context because pastors are held to a higher standard, so it's even more shocking and damaging when trust is lost.

Trust is foundational. Without it, a ReLeader can never rebuild. Seth Godin said, "Earn trust, earn trust, earn trust. Then you can worry about the rest."[3]

The trouble is that you can't microwave trust. It takes time.

That's why, while I feel I was led to ask the people at Victory Church to credit trust to me, it couldn't happen in a day. I had to earn it.

You build trust slowly. There's no magic bullet, but if you want my *Building Trust for Dummies* advice, I'd say you do what you say you're going to do, repeatedly, over the course of time.

I know this: If you can't build trust, you can't be a ReLeader.

Any leader can spend time in an organization and see the issues and challenges at hand and even know how to bring correction. But great leaders are those who know that making those moves without trust is like turning a cruise ship as though it were a speedboat. You can turn quickly, but you'll push most of the people off your boat, and those who remain will be incredibly nauseated.

When I stepped into the role of lead pastor, building the congregation's trust was at the top of my list. The only way I knew how to do that was by communicating with transparency and authenticity. In the spring of 2015, I watched the State of the Union address given by the president of the United States. And while I questioned whether or not presidents have been transparent or authentic, I understood the purpose of the event. It was to let the American public know the health of our nation and what the president planned to do to improve it. So in the spring of 2015, I did my very first State of the Church address in front of the entire church on a Sunday morning.

This involved going into the details and status of the inner workings of our church over the previous year, where we stood at the moment, and where I saw us going in the future. I was straightforward, talking about things they had never heard a pastor address. I talked about things such as:

- How the lead pastor's salary is set.
- What the makeup of our church board was like.
- The balance of our church's debt load and the status of our debt-to-income ratio.
- What our total budget was for the previous year and whether or not we had a balanced budget.
- I described the audit our church finances went through each year.

- I explained that I do not travel alone.
- I shared who my pastors are and whom I am accountable to.

Our people were completely floored that a pastor would give such details about his life and the inner workings of their church. I wanted them to know this was a house that they could trust, where their families would be safe, and that would provide fertile soil for them to plant their seeds of time, talent, and treasure.

I've taken criticism for being so transparent over the years from other pastors and leaders, and I'm not saying it's a model for everyone to follow. There are limitations to what I share and what I don't. But I can tell you that candid communication has built a solid foundation of trust that has allowed me to make some strong moves throughout my years as the lead pastor. For those who "credited me trust" in those early years, I have done everything in my power to pay it back, and I am deeply grateful for them.

BUILD PEOPLE

One of the more challenging components of ReLeading is that you did not hire your staff. You didn't choose or train them. Instead, before you arrived, the culture of the organization molded and shaped them. And since you're having to rebuild, chances are that culture is questionable at best.

I love the book *Good to Great* by Jim Collins.[4] Borrowing his language, one of your first priorities as a ReLeader is to make sure the right people are on the bus and that they're in the right seats.

When I stepped into my position as the new lead pastor, there were tremendous amounts of pain, feelings of betrayal, and confusion among the staff. In the few months I was serving as the interim lead pastor, the previous lead pastor's wife was the chair of the board, and even into my becoming the lead pastor, there were several members of their family still on staff. These are leadership paths that are littered with mine fields that could take off a leg with any wrong step. If you are a ReLeader, you're very familiar with such mine fields.

Let me just tell you: there *will be* turnover. I wasn't naive; I knew there would be turnover in our staff. Some would probably leave by choice, and there were others I would need to let go. It's not fun, but the buck stops with the ReLeader.

One particular family member of the former lead pastor was not happy with me. He had been promised a leadership role in the church prior to D-Day (the name we later gave to the day all hell broke loose when the moral failure became public). He had moved his entire family from another state and arrived to discover the role he had been promised was not going to be given to him. I had to walk him through that pain and help him transition to the next chapter of his life.

You will have many such bloody and painful meetings. Think of each one as another chiseled block that you are placing in the foundation as you rebuild the organization you are called to ReLead.

Through my experience—and a lot of wisdom I gleaned from others—I learned some important lessons on building the foundation of people in your organization. Here are three:

Pick Carefully

Toward the beginning of His ministry, Jesus chose 12 people to be His team. Before making those selections, He spent an entire night praying (see Luke 6:12). He was careful because He knew how important it was.

These first few years you will lay the essential building blocks for your entire time in this role, and whom you surround yourself with will either make or break your ReLeader journey.

I frequently talk to leaders who are in this process of trying to get the right people in the right seats on the bus. Here's some advice I give as someone who has walked this path before.

Get your leadership team in place quickly.

You will more than likely need to make several staff changes over the next few years, and you want a leadership team to partner with you in those decisions. We know the best decisions happen when they're infused with lots of wise counsel.

Lead with people you love.

You should love doing life with your leadership team. I'm not saying they have to be your best buddies, and yes, you will have disagreements, but you need to love being together. Chemistry is critical.

But what if you inherit a leadership team? Spend two to three months trying to determine whether you have the right chemistry. If not, you will need to make changes. How and when you make these moves is precarious. If you do it without love or compassion, or wait too long or act too quickly, it can have devastating consequences for your trust and equity with the staff. So how do you make sure you do it right? Follow Jesus' example and spend the night in prayer. Ask the Holy Spirit to guide you. When you know, act swiftly but in a pastoral manner. The longer you wait, the more difficult it will become.

Staff your weaknesses.

Your team should share your vision but possess a very different set of giftings and skills.

For example, I am not great with details, nor am I interested in contemplating or debriefing. I am so future focused that I miss a lot of details and can fail to learn from past mistakes. I can't let my weaknesses become our organization's weaknesses, so I have to surround myself with people who are strong where I am weak.

Keep your leadership team small.

Depending on the size of your organization, you may have just a few, dozens, or hundreds of staff members, but regardless, I suggest keeping your leadership team to only three to five trusted people.

At Victory Church, our Directional Leadership Team has only four members, including me.

During my time at The King's University, I had five on my President's Cabinet, including me.

Regardless of what you call it, the team closest to you needs to be relatively small.

You might ask why. Some reasons are logistical. A smaller team means less difficulty juggling everyone's calendars for meetings, retreats, and the occasional pop-up gathering.

Also, in my experience, the more people in the room, the more opportunities you have for bottlenecks in the decision-making process and the ultimate advancement of your organization. If you are looking for more insights, input, ideas, or perspectives, consider bringing in people with those gifts to give wisdom to and consult with your leadership, but they do not need to be a part of the team or the decision-making process.

Develop layers of leadership.

Jesus had His "top three" leaders—Peter, James, and John—as well as the other nine disciples (for a total of 12). We also see Him appointing 72 leaders to go out and minister (see Luke 10).

In Acts there seems to be the top level leadership of the apostles, but in Acts 6 we see they need to give their "attention to prayer and the ministry of the word." So they choose seven leaders to whom they give an important ministry assignment.

Creating a second tier of leadership gives ownership and authority further down in the organization. At both The King's University and Victory Church, I created the Strategic Leadership Team (SLT). This helped empower a level of leadership to take "tasks of distraction" off the leadership team so they can focus on bigger picture items. Having a second tier of leadership also pushes decision-making further down into the organization and frees up the top tier leadership team to focus on bigger things. It can also provide chances for others to step into leadership roles to use their gifts and abilities in greater ways. It should improve the retention of sharp leaders in your organization as it creates layers of leadership development and opportunity.

If you have individuals on the leadership team you inherited whom you decide are not the right fit and need to be removed, a secondary leadership team can provide a softer landing.

You may be paralyzed by the fear that you might make a mistake in hiring or in moving people in your organization, but don't waste time worrying. Yes, it may happen, but remember that even Jesus had one of His 12 who didn't work out.

Pack Patience

If you're a ReLeader, patience is more than a virtue—it's like dialysis for someone with kidney failure. You can't live without it. That's why my wife Michele often says to me, "Pack your patience." You pack a lunch because you know you'll get hungry, and then you unpack it to quench the hunger.

Why do you pack patience? Because you'll need it.

Patience is not a strength of mine. My friend Dr. Sam Chand says, "Fire quickly and hire slowly." Looking back, I'm not sure I always got this right. In 90 percent of leadership cases, I completely agree with Dr. Chand. However, in a ReLeader's first few years, they do not always get the luxury of firing quickly. Every organization is different, and each brings with it a unique and challenging set of circumstances. When you take a ReLeader role, it comes with tons of baggage, and land mines are everywhere. Typically, lines have been drawn in the sand, and everyone has chosen a side. Each decision you make as a ReLeader can—and many times *will*—cause even more division. You'll be able to make some decisions without creating chaos, but there will be other decisions—perhaps a necessary firing—that you can't make until you've earned some trust in the organization. But trust does not come easily or quickly, especially for those called to fix what they didn't break. So pack your patience.

Trust does not come easily or quickly, especially for those called to fix what they didn't break. So pack your patience.

Pray Often

Can I be honest? Sometimes prayer may not seem very practical or results oriented. Yes, I know it's vital, but when I need to take action, prayer can feel like a restraint.

But it's not.

Prayer is our most powerful weapon as ReLeaders. We need to pray continually. Many people turn most naturally to prayer when they're up against the wall. ReLeaders are *often* up against the wall, so prayer should come easier for us.

You already know this, but powerful things happen when you pray. And often the most powerful impact is on *you*. I love how Philippians 4:6–7 reads in *The Message*: "Don't fret or worry. Instead of worrying, pray. Let petitions and praises shape your worries into prayers, letting God know your concerns. Before you know it, a sense of God's wholeness, everything coming together for good, will come and settle you down."

My pastor, Craig Groeschel, always says, "If it's big enough to worry about, it's big enough to pray about." I wrote in Chapter 4 about three prayers I would pray every night before I went to bed. Those prayers were reminders that God had entrusted me with the position He put me in and the organization He had me leading. And I hope you know that if God has entrusted you to be a ReLeader, then He trusts you. Let that sink in. The Creator of the universe has appointed you and trusts you. That is amazing—and intimidating—so pray often and keep moving forward, keeping in step with the Holy Spirit.

I don't think I've ever prayed more than I did in my first few years as a ReLeader. I started so many days on my face in my living room before my family got out of bed. I remember one particular season when I had a staff member who was creating all kinds of problems. He was challenging my every move, going from office to office spewing toxic waste. But because of some political and relational circumstances, firing this person would have been the equivalent of detonating a nuclear bomb. What did I do? I set my alarm for 5 am, got on my face, and asked God to intervene. Just six hours later, immediately following an all-staff meeting, this person was in my office giving me the business. Then the Holy Spirit showed up and gave me a word that softened and shifted the entire conversation. No, not "You're fired" or "Straighten up or else." I said, "I am so sorry this happened to you." Those prayer-induced, Holy Spirit-led words broke down the walls of a hardened heart, and this person began to weep. Within moments this person asked what I thought they should do. I said, "I think you should resign." And just like that, it was resolved. *Prayer* did that.

There are some things you *can* do. After all, you're a great leader, and God has already given you wisdom, empowerment, and resolve. But there are other things that are not by might, nor by power, but by His Spirit (see Zechariah 4:6).

In Mark 9, the disciples approached Jesus to tell Him they attempted to cast out a demon but fell short of their goal. It was one thing they just could *not* do. How did Jesus reply to them? "This kind cannot come out by anything but prayer" (v. 29 NASB1995). Can I encourage you, as you ReLead, to be quick to learn the things in your organization that can only come by prayer? You want to build a strong foundation, so pray often.

BUILD SYSTEMS

You've built trust. You've built people. Last, but certainly not least, you have to build systems.

We do not get much detail about *how* Zerubbabel and Jeshua rebuilt the foundation, but they must have put some systems in place. We do get a few more specifics in the case of Solomon's foundation buildout:

> Solomon had seventy thousand carriers and eighty thousand stonecutters in the hills, as well as thirty-three hundred foremen who supervised the project and directed the workers. At the king's command they removed from the quarry large blocks of high-grade stone to provide a foundation of dressed stone for the temple (1 Kings 5:15–17).

We see words like supervised, directed, command, and removed. We see roles such as stonecutters, supervisors, directors, and kings. Solomon put systems in place, and they created results. The text says the result of these systems "provided a foundation of dressed stone for the Temple."

You *must* have effective systems. But what if you're not the Pastor Chris Hodges of systems? (If you're not aware, you could be "the Michael Jordan of basketball" or "the Elon Musk of electric cars" or "the Chris Hodges of systems." Chris is *amazing* with systems!) If you're not, that doesn't mean your rebuilding project is doomed to fail. You don't have to create the systems, but you *are* the one who must ensure your organization has them.

Honestly, I am not a great systems guy. Details are not my thing (if my leadership teams are reading this, then they might have just laughed out loud a little bit). Words like "policies" and "procedures" send chills down my spine. Even typing those words caused my face to twitch. But make no mistake, I fully understand how vitally important they are to the health of any organization.

If, like me, you're not a systems leader, that's okay. Find someone who is and put them by your side because you must build systems to repair the foundation of your organization.

JUST GET STARTED

You now have some specific direction on three priority foundation-building actions, but even so, you may be screaming at this book, "But where do I start?"

I remember starting the process of my doctoral dissertation. The coursework was easy. Lectures, reading, assignments with step-by-step instructions, feedback, and expectations from the professor—those were a piece of cake. Then the dissertation process began. There were broad instructions, but depending on your chosen dissertation type, the specifics were scarce. And deadlines—what deadlines? It was all on you. So where was I supposed to start?

I've found writing a book to be similar. You have a broad concept and a few outlines here and there, but where do you start?

Do you know the answer?

No?

Good news, then, because I have the answer for you.

You just get started.

With a dissertation? Just get started.

Writing a book? Sit down, stare at that blinking cursor on the blank page, and begin typing.

ReLeading? Yep. Just get started.

Zerubbabel and Jeshua couldn't pull out the yellow pages or do a Google search to find a local contractor in the Jerusalem area. They couldn't go down to the local Home Depot and buy all the materials they needed. They didn't have the gold and silver or the tens of thousands of workers Solomon had. Nor would they have Solomon's influence with surrounding nations.

So what should they do?

Just get started.

Begin the work and then watch God work.

> In the second month of the second year after their arrival at the house of God in Jerusalem, Zerubbabel son of Shealtiel, Joshua son of Jozadak and the rest of the people (the priests and the Levites and

> all who had returned from the captivity to Jerusalem) *began the work* (Ezra 3:8, italics added).

They began the work. The Hebrew word for began in this text is *nāṣaḥ* (pronounced *naw-tsakh'*). It means 'to excel, be bright, be the overseer, or be enduring.' That was the charge to Zerubbabel, Jeshua, and the rest of the Israelites—they were to begin the work, and to excel and endure in it.

That's what God has called *you* to when He sparked your enthusiasm. You have everything you need to do the work. You know what's required of you and have the reassurance of a loving and limitless God. So even if it's just a small first step, you can begin the work. I love Zechariah 4:10: "Do not despise these small beginnings, for the LORD rejoices to see the work begin" (NLT). What you can do right now might seem insignificant and small. But what does the Lord rejoice to see? You might assume God would rejoice most when He sees the work completed. That's what we've been trained to celebrate. But this text tells us God rejoices to see the work *begin*. When you are hesitatingly taking your first fledgling steps, God is throwing a party, celebrating the beginning of your work.

When you are hesitatingly taking
your first fledgling steps,
God is throwing a party,
celebrating the beginning of your work.

The Remnant

Ezra 3:8 lists the people involved in this rebuild. Ezra, of course, names the leaders, Zerubbabel and Jeshua. Then Ezra mentions "the rest of the people." The KJV calls them "the remnant." Remnant comes from the Hebrew word *šᵊ'ār* (pronounced *sheh-awr'*), which means 'the rest, the residue, or that which remains.'

This was one of the most arduous lessons of my ReLeader journey, and I hope to help you avoid some of the pain of my mistakes. What I failed to realize about the remnant at Victory Church is that I had no control over who was part of the remnant and who wasn't.

Who makes up the remnant? Those who make the decision to come back and rebuild.

Who decides who's a part of the remnant? The remnant decides.

The remnant is the group of individuals who decide to remain. Did you notice there's no indication Zerubbabel and Jeshua ran around recruiting and begging people to join the remnant? Ezra never mentioned that they took people out for steaks, or baked chocolate chip cookies, or offered box seats to games if only people would become part of the remnant.

I suffered many sleepless nights trying to plan out the remnant in my mind. Like a guy preparing for his fantasy football draft, I decided who I wanted for each leadership position, assessing their gifts, talents, and, quite frankly, their giving potential. I became obsessed and overwhelmed with who had left and who might be leaving. For several months, these compulsive and faithless thoughts dominated my mind and took me to dreadful places emotionally.

Leaders are great visionaries who are gifted to plan the future in their minds. But unfortunately, that can also be a curse. If we're not careful, we will get out in front of God. At our best we are planning, but at our worst we're scheming. Sometimes it's hard for leaders to tell the difference. I need to accept that there are some things I cannot control, and the remnant is one of them. I finally realized that when it comes to the remnant, God wanted His job back.

Yet again, it was Pastor Jimmy Evans who gave me some incredible insights in this area. I will warn you; it is a little crass, but it drove the point home for me. Jimmy explained to me that in nature every organism takes in sustenance, benefits from what it needs to benefit from, and then excretes what it does not need. He explained that, in this way, organizations are similar. An organization is, in a way, a living, breathing organism. It is nourished and sustained by the people in it. Occasionally, someone will leave, and we must trust that it's God's timing that they're no longer beneficial and therefore must be excreted. I was taking all that in (no pun intended) when Jimmy looked me in the eye and asked, "Jon, after your body excreted something, did you ever pick it up and eat it?" (Sorry, I know it's gross, but stay with me). "No," I replied, "of course not." Then, in true Jimmy fashion, he said, "Then stop going around begging people to be a part of your remnant. Trust God and work with what you've got in front of you."

If we're not careful,
we will get out in front of God.

Wow!

God was teaching me the invaluable lesson I first mentioned in Chapter 1: Don't focus on who left, focus on who is left.

Remember in Chapter 1 we looked at the story in Judges 6 where God had Gideon whittle down his army from 32,000 to 300. I wish the text went into detail about Gideon's mindset through this process. I'm not sure if he was filled with anxiety or faith, but I know Gideon learned what every ReLeader learns: I don't get to play a part in the *size* of the remnant, but I do get to play a part in the *impact* of the remnant.

It is not your job to choose who's in or the size of the remnant. Your role is to be faithful with the people God gives you and to build the impact you and the remnant can have together.

Stop and Celebrate the Wins

It's confession time.

When we go on a family road trip, I love typing the destination into the GPS. But it's not because I don't know where I'm going or want to see where we're going. I love the moment I put the destination into the GPS because that's when I get the estimated time of arrival—the ETA—and I just *know* I can beat it. The GPS will declare, "Time of arrival: 5:51," and I look at my wife, smile, and say, "Wanna bet?"

Yes, I've got issues.

My personality type is "Driven." When I see a challenge, I set a goal, and I start chasing after it.

On a road trip, that's a good trait for arriving a few minutes early, but it's a terrible trait for everyone else in the car with me. They are terrified to ask to go to the bathroom (because the answer is always, "You can hold it!"). Plus, my driving can be erratic, and heaven forbid we enjoy the journey by stopping to create a few special moments.

That's not only the way I drive; it's also the easiest way for me to lead. I can become so dead set on accomplishing a task that I make it a miserable ride for everyone else in the organization.

I've had to learn that this is *not* the best way to lead, and one person who taught me that is Ezra:

> When the builders laid the foundation of the temple of the Lord, the priests in their vestments and with trumpets, and the Levites (the sons of Asaph) with cymbals, *took their places to praise the* Lord, as prescribed by David king of Israel. *With praise and thanksgiving they sang to the* Lord:
>
> "He is good;
> his love toward Israel endures forever."
>
> And all *the people gave a great shout of praise* to the Lord, because the foundation of the house of the Lord was laid (Ezra 3:10–11, italics added).

I've come to understand that the goal of getting to the destination as quickly as possible is *not* godly. We need to stop along the way.

The work of building the Temple came to a halt for one reason—to *celebrate*. They weren't finished. They were just getting started. The amount of work still to be done was overwhelming, but even still they pushed pause with a purpose—to celebrate a win. They gave a great shout of praise because the foundation of the house of the Lord was laid.

About a year into my leadership role at TKU, our admissions team hit some of their recruiting goals, and I wanted to get everyone together for a quick celebration. I told my executive assistant to call a meeting outside my office and tell the whole staff to come over. I later found out that when the announcement was made, many of the staff were afraid that some big layoffs were going to be made. What was planned was a celebration, but it was received as something fear-inducing. That revealed to me that our organization's history created a culture of not celebrating wins. But I have devoted myself, and encourage you, to be a leader who celebrates small beginnings and small wins.

If you are "celebration-impaired" like me, then here are a few ways you can do better:

- Intentionally celebrate things that are harder to measure, like changed lives.
- Create a recurring segment for your all-staff gatherings in which you spend time letting members of your team share wins from their departments.
- Determine "leading indicators" that lead toward your big wins. In other words, what small steps move forward to the big wins? It will then be easier to identify what small things to celebrate.
- Consider delegating celebrations to someone else. (You could call that person the CPO: Chief Partying Officer.)

Noise from Naysayers

Picture it: The foundation for the Temple is now set. People are overjoyed and celebrating. God is being praised. The work can continue unhindered.

What do you think happens next?

It's what often happens next for ReLeaders in rebuilding efforts. Check out what happens after the people gave a great shout of praise:

> And all the people gave a great shout of praise to the LORD, because the foundation of the house of the LORD was laid. But many of the older priests and Levites and family heads, who had seen the former temple, wept aloud when they saw the foundation of this temple being laid, while many others shouted for joy. No one could distinguish the sound of the shouts of joy from the sound of weeping, because the people made so much noise. And the sound was heard far away (Ezra 3:11–13).

A leadership storm was brewing.

Remember, we've learned there is a former house and a present house, and there will always be those who still love the former house. It's understandable, because the former house was amazing.

Why exactly were the older people weeping? We find out it's because they had seen the former Temple. What's interesting is that the Hebrew word for weeping in this text is *bāḵâ* (pronounced *baw-kaw'*), which can mean weeping from either grief or joy. Perhaps the older remnant had mixed emotions. On one hand, they are thrilled to see the Temple being rebuilt and are weeping with joy. Yet they also remember it in its former state. They can't forget the stunning beauty, the great signs of wealth, the lavish amenities. They look at the new Temple and realize it's not the same—and they are *not* happy about it.

Verse 13 describes well what ReLeadership feels like at times: "No one could distinguish the sound of the shouts of joy from the sound of weeping, because the people made so much noise." My dad was a pastor for 22 years and has often joked, "Son, pastoring would be really easy if it weren't for the people." If you've pastored or led people in any capacity, you figured out pretty quickly that sheep bite.

In my ReLeader adventure, most of my decisions were met with rejoicing *and* weeping. The decisions of ReLeaders are especially subject to being met with weeping because the people in your remnant have history with the organization from long before you arrived. They saw the former house in all its glory, long before it crumbled. During that time of glory, they drew conclusions about how and why the success was happening. Then you come in, and many of your decisions war against their conclusions. What is the end result? Conflict!

ReLeaders need to remember that someone being a part of the remnant does not mean they want to rebuild with the same set of blueprints.

For Zerubbabel and Jeshua, it was only the beginning of the conflict. In fact, from this point until Nehemiah completes the wall around Jerusalem, there is basically nothing but conflict. It reaches a point in Ezra 4 when it seems as if *everyone* is against them. There was conflict internally, in their region and with the government overseers.

Not only were people weeping, but in chapter 4, some of the locals become adversaries. People who claimed to want to help in the rebuild were actually trying to stop the work. Zerubbabel and Jeshua—perhaps because they had leadership intuition—declined their offer to help, and then these people revealed their true colors.

> Then the peoples around them set out to discourage the people of Judah and make them afraid to go on building. They bribed officials to work against them and frustrate their plans during the entire reign of Cyrus king of Persia and down to the reign of Darius king of Persia (Ezra 4:4–5).

I know you don't want to hear this, but in your ReLeader book, you'll have a few chapters of conflict too. The closer you get to the work being completed, the more the enemy will take notice.

For Zerubbabel and Jeshua, their conflict led to the halting of the work.

> As soon as the copy of the letter of King Artaxerxes was read to Rehum and Shimshai the secretary and their associates, they went immediately to the Jews in Jerusalem and compelled them by force to stop.
>
> Thus the work on the house of God in Jerusalem came to a standstill until the second year of the reign of Darius king of Persia (Ezra 4:23–24).

Perhaps you're in a chapter where you feel like stopping the work. You received the call, you started, you're in the middle of your rebuild, but you feel like there are too many things trying to stop you.

If you're in a chapter filled with conflict, and the work has "come to a standstill," then the next chapter is for you.

7

REmain

SEVENTEEN YEARS OF NOTHING

Seventeen years is a long time.

As I write this book, it's toward the end of 2023, so 17 years ago was 2006. Let me take you back.

In 2006:

- I was a spry 26 years old.
- My daughter was minus 1 year old, and my son was minus 4 (a.k.a., not yet a twinkle in their daddy's eye).
- Facebook had just changed its name from *The Facebook* and opened membership from only high school and college students to anyone over the age of 13.
- Twitter did not exist. Neither did Kindle or Airbnb.
- Blu-ray discs and iPod Nanos were brand new.
- The cost of a gallon of gas was about $2.30 and a dozen eggs $1.30.
- The big movies were *Night at the Museum* and *Cars.*
- Shakira was singing that her *Hips Don't Lie.*
- *Time Magazine's* "Person of the Year" was "You"—all the people who were now using the World Wide Web.

Seventeen years is a long time ... to do nothing.

WALKING AWAY

Have you ever played Chutes and Ladders with your kids? You work your way through a path on the board. You're making progress. You have moments of momentum on steroids as you climb ladders. *But then.* Then there are the crashes where you are shooting down a chute and progress is lost, and you just want to grab the game board, throw it against a wall, and storm out of the room. (I may take kids' games too seriously.)

Chutes and Ladders would be fine (a little frustrating but fine) if it were just a board game. The problem is that it's way too much like ReLeading.

Zerubbabel and Jeshua are well on their way to rebuilding the Temple. The altar is in place on its original spot, and they've laid the foundation of the Temple. They have overcome so much.

Have you been there? Healing is starting to happen. People are beginning to get it. Core values have been written, printed, and communicated. Team members are even mentioning them. You finally see some progress.

Do you know what happens next?

Hint: It's *not* good.

Invariably, after progress there is regress. After momentum there is *slow*mentum. After encouragement, there is discouragement. Somewhere along the path, often after a mountaintop moment, you are confronted by difficult people, financial hardship, and oppressive circumstances. You go from confused to dismayed to just wanting to walk away.

That's what's next for Zerubbabel and Jeshua, and we should take note of *when* it happens: just after they finished the foundation and just before the structure started going vertical.

I have a friend who just finished building a large, three-story building off the highway in Southlake, Texas. When they were cutting into the dirt, laying the plumbing work, and pouring the foundation, no one could see the work from the road. But once the walls started going vertical, everyone noticed.

I wonder if the enemy is not too concerned with our work in the fledgling phases, but when it goes vertical, he comes at us like a hurricane.

Sometimes he comes as a hurricane disguised as help.

That is exactly what happens with Zerubbabel and Jeshua. We read in Ezra 4 that some locals offered to come alongside and assist in the Temple construction. Zerubbabel and Jeshua, with great discernment, declined their offer. They knew there was something off with these guys, and they were correct. They were not friends but enemies with bad intentions.

> Then the peoples around them set out to discourage the people of Judah and make them afraid to go on building. They bribed officials to work against them and frustrate their plans during the entire reign of Cyrus king of Persia and down to the reign of Darius king of Persia (Ezra 4:4–5).

The discouragement is extreme, and it more than slows down progress. The work came to a screeching stop. "Thus the work on the house of God in Jerusalem came to a standstill until the second year of the reign of Darius king of Persia" (Ezra 4:24).

The discouragement for Zerubbabel and Jeshua was so oppressive that they completely walked away from their calling.

They did not take a day off. They didn't go to Cabo for a week on the beach.

How long was the stoppage?

Sometimes the date of a particular event in the Bible is revealed, not by giving us a year in the text but by naming who was reigning as king. During this time there were no kings in Israel, but the dates can be estimated through the foreign kings ruling at the time. Historians differ in their conclusion as to the total length of this delay, but most follow a timeline that has the work delayed at somewhere between 15 and 18 years.[1] One scholar estimates the work was halted in 537 BC and picked back up again in 520 BC. So ... 17 years. And we've already established that 17 years is a long time, especially to do nothing.

We might judge Zerubbabel and Jeshua for walking away from their calling, but I think we understand because there are days for all of us when it seems easier to just walk away.

Can I be honest? There are days I drive home from a hard day of ministry and look with envy at the guy running a bulldozer on the side of the road. I love the idea of clocking in, seeing instant progress come from the work of my hands, and then clocking out, not having to worry about it again until tomorrow. Or maybe I could get a job at an ice cream shop. I don't think people ever oppose someone giving them two scoops or a banana split. But ministry is hard. It never ends. People are often unhappy because of decisions you make. And you're not just a leader. You are a preacher, staff manager, drama extinguisher, fundraiser, vision caster, CEO, CFO, and the biggest job of all, CPS (Chief Problem Solver). I think every pastor fires themselves on Monday and then gains the courage to rehire themselves on Tuesday. And Sundays keep coming—at an alarming rate. Just when you walk off the stage after pouring your guts out, you start all over, knowing you have to write a sermon just as good as the one the week before or people will decide to get fed somewhere else. And if that wasn't enough, it all becomes magnified and more complicated if you're a ReLeader in a rebuild.

So I have a hard time blaming Zerubbabel and Jeshua for walking away. I'm not saying they did the right thing, but I get it.

REIGNITE THE FIRE

I'm not bold enough to guarantee many things. I fill out my bracket for the NCAA Tournament like the next guy, have my best guess for who will win the Super Bowl, and occasionally feel confident about a stock—but I'm wrong more than I'm right.

However, I *am* bold enough to guarantee that if you are a ReLeader, you will face moments of discouragement so dark that you will be tempted to walk away.

Like Clubber Lang said in *Rocky III,* "My prediction? Pain."

So what does God do when leaders want to quit on their calling? He intervenes. God does not do it by coming in and doing the work. He intervenes by creating a second spark.

If you go camping and need a fire, but the one you started burns out, then you don't go home. You restart the fire.

God chose Zerubbabel and Jeshua. He gave them a spark of enthusiasm. Discouragement sucked the oxygen out of these two ReLeaders, and the spark was extinguished. But God does not ridicule them. He doesn't cancel them and find someone else to finish the work. No, He sends a prophet to reignite the fire. God sends His Word to refresh and renew the divine calling to finish the work.

> Then he said to me, "This is what the LORD says to Zerubbabel: It is not by force nor by strength, but by my Spirit, says the LORD of Heaven's Armies. Nothing, not even a mighty mountain, will stand in Zerubbabel's way; it will become a level plain before him! And when Zerubbabel sets the final stone of the Temple in place, the people will shout: 'May God bless it! May God bless it!'"
>
> Then another message came to me from the LORD: "Zerubbabel is the one who laid the foundation of this Temple, and he will complete it. Then you will know that the LORD of Heaven's Armies has sent me. Do not despise these small beginnings, for the LORD rejoices to see the work begin, to see the plumb line in Zerubbabel's hand" (Zechariah 4:6–10 NLT).

There is a theological word to describe this speech: *Dang!*

We talked about locker room speeches, and this has to be one of the greatest halftime pep talks of all time!

God gives a word to Zerubbabel and to every ReLeader who would come after him. God reminds Zerubbabel that, from the beginning, this was a God-assignment.

Remember, at this point around 17 years have passed. When I think about 17 years ago, I struggle to remember much. At this point, rebuilding the Temple is probably just a faint memory for Zerubbabel. I bet his failure had haunted him—for nearly two decades! The regret and shame had to be overwhelming.

That experience may resonate with you.

That's why I am so thankful we serve a God of second chances.

Fix What You Broke

Throughout this book I've said ReLeaders are called to fix what they did not break. That's true, but ... ReLeaders sometimes mess up too.

God originally called Zerubbabel to rebuild the Temple. After a strong start, he quit. And now God was giving him a chance to *re*-ReLead.

ReLeaders fix what they did not break, but sometimes they're called to fix what they *did* break.

Chances are, you've messed up. Well, when I say that, I'm assuming something. I'm assuming you're human. If so, you've probably done one or more of these things:

- Messed up some things in your business.
- In an honest moment, your spouse might say you've messed up some things in your marriage.
- Your kids may mention you once or twice in future counseling appointments because you haven't parented them perfectly.
- And it's likely you've made some leadership moves that caused more problems than they've solved.

Here's the good news: Instead of giving up on us, God gives us opportunities to fix what we *did* break.

I feel the need to add this: Sometimes the broken thing that needs to be fixed is *in* us. It may be something broken in you has contributed to some of the damage you've done. You might even feel broken beyond repair. But that's not true. If ReLeaders fix things they didn't break, then God is the ultimate ReLeader because He is faithful to fix the broken things in us.

As a ReLeader you will reach a point, if you haven't already, in which you will break something and be tempted to walk away. But remember, if it were easy, everyone would do it. And you *can* do hard things. God wants to give you the strength to finish the important work in front of you. We serve a redeeming God who will renew, not revoke, the call on your life.

Instead of giving up on us,
God gives us opportunities to fix
what we did *break.*

I am so thankful for this story in the Bible, and I believe God's message to Zerubbabel, spoken through the prophet Zechariah, is a prophetic word to every ReLeader who will listen and receive it. For the remainder of this chapter, I want to break this passage down verse by verse, pull out every ounce of encouragement, and deposit all of it into your spirit.

YOUR STRENGTH WON'T CUT IT

When my kids were very little—I'm talking two to four years old—I would make them help me carry the grocery bags after arriving home from the store. After giving them the lightest bag, we would take off on the long, terrifying journey of 30 steps to the kitchen. Inevitably, about five steps in, they would turn to me and say, "Daddy, it's too heavy ... HELP!" I did what any dad would do: I would swoop in, take the load from them, and carry all the groceries in myself (every real man can get all the bags in one trip). As their father, it was never my intention to cause them agony but to allow them to partner with their father in doing an important work. We all knew that, at any time, they could turn to their dad, and I would take the weight from them.

God had a similar word for Zerubbabel after he had dropped his grocery bag 17 years prior to this moment.

Let's look at the very first words God delivers to Zerubbabel:

> Then he said to me, "This is what the LORD says to Zerubbabel: *It is not by force nor by strength, but by my Spirit,* says the LORD of Heaven's Armies" (Zechariah 4:6 NLT, italics added).

This is a popular verse. You've preached it or heard it in a sermon or seen it on a coffee mug. "Not by force nor by strength, but by my Spirit." It's interpreted as an encouraging word, and it is, but what if it's also a correction?

ReLeaders tend to be very gifted and take their calling very personally, and so they can unintentionally leave God out of it. Isn't that crazy? We are called by God, driven by our love of God, doing it for God, and yet we can leave God out and go it alone.

There are some things you can do by force. (I can force myself to eat an entire pizza in one sitting if you dare me). There are other things you can do by strength. (I can hit a golf ball 300 or more yards. It may not always be straight.) But I think God is reminding Zerubbabel that some things are above our pay grade. Some things are in God's job description, not ours.

As a ReLeader, there are things you do with your hands and feet, and then there are other things you do on your knees.

As a ReLeader, there are things you do with your hands and feet, and then there are other things you do on your knees.

Jesus reminded the disciples of this in Mark 9. I mentioned this story in the last chapter, when the disciples came to Jesus, flustered by a situation where they were unable to drive a demon out of a young boy. After all, wasn't this exactly the kind of thing Jesus had instructed them to do? What is going on when you can't do what God has called you to do? Jesus answered them, "This kind can come out only by prayer" (Mark 9:29). Some manuscripts included "and fasting." In any case, prayer is essential in the process. If I understand correctly, Jesus is saying they tried to drive out a demon without even praying! That sounds insane, and I can't imagine it—except sometimes that describes the way I've done ministry.

Jesus was saying to His disciples what the prophet Zechariah said to Zerubbabel, that some things are not by might, nor by power, but only by the Spirit of God.

As a ReLeader, there will be times when your strength just won't cut it. It will be difficult to discern when you need to pick something up and when you need to lay it down. When the burden is too heavy to lift or carry, it can feel tempting to follow in the path of Zerubbabel and quit your job. But instead, I encourage you to give God His job back.

When you work for someone else, you receive a job description that lays out a clear picture of the expectations by which your work will be measured. In the same way, you have a God-given ReLeader job description. God also has a job description. When you try to do tasks that are only in God's job description, things will go haywire, and you'll feel like you're being crushed by the weight of it all. Do you know why? *Because you ain't God.* You can't do what only God can do. Your qualifications fall well short of what it takes to fulfill His role.

Here are a few passages that clue us in to God's responsibilities and remind us how ridiculous and prideful it is for us to try to take them on:

> In his hand are the depths of the earth,
> and the mountain peaks belong to him.
> The sea is his, for he made it,
> and his hands formed the dry land (Psalm 95:4–5).

> Have you not known?
> Have you not heard?
> The everlasting God, the LORD,

> The creator of the ends of the earth,
> Neither faints nor is weary.
> His understanding is unsearchable.
> He gives power to the weak,
> And to *those who have* no might He increases strength.
> Even the youths shall faint and be weary,
> And the young men shall utterly fall,
> But those who wait on the LORD
> Shall renew *their* strength;
> They shall mount up with wings like eagles,
> They shall run and not be weary,
> They shall walk and not faint (Isaiah 40:28–31 NKJV).

> For in him all things were created: things in heaven and on earth, visible and invisible, whether thrones or powers or rulers or authorities; all things have been created through him and for him. He is before all things, and in him all things hold together (Colossians 1:16–17).

I think you get it.

If you are feeling discouraged, if you're stressed out or burned out, if you're considering quitting, then could it be that you're working outside of your job description? And instead of walking away, you need to give God His job back.

- Maybe you're too focused on growing a big church and less focused on growing big people?
- You might be too focused on finding new leaders when God is asking you to develop the ones in front of you?
- Perhaps you're trying to change your spouse. Can I just tell you that is *way* outside of your job description?
- You might find yourself writing and rewriting and perfecting and memorizing your sermon—but never really praying about it.
- Could it be you're too focused on becoming wealthy when God is asking you to focus on stewarding what you already have?

I don't know what you're facing, but I challenge you to do a serious review of your job description. Ask the Lord what you've put in your job description that belongs in His. Some things are not by your might, nor by your power, but only by His Spirit.

GOD IS FOR YOU

Growing up, I was always "Andy's little brother." Andy is my older brother and was always my hero! Because he is two years older than me, I've always followed in his footsteps. When I went to junior high, I was "Andy's little brother." When I got to high school, I was "Andy's little brother." Even when I got to college where we played basketball together, I was still "Andy's little brother." Because of that, I always had friends, I always had favor, and most importantly, I always had protection. Why? Because my big brother was always "for me."

In this ReLeader adventure you've embarked on, who is for you really matters, and I would love to sit down with you and share just four words:

God is for you.

That fact changes everything!

God is for you.

He is!

- He called you, didn't He?
- He gave you the spark of enthusiasm for this task, didn't He?
- He entrusted it to you, didn't He?

I absolutely love Zechariah 4:7. Even after Zerubbabel walked away and sat on the sidelines for nearly 20 years, God gave him a word of empowerment and encouragement that would get anyone off the bench and into the game:

> Nothing, not even a mighty mountain, will stand in Zerubbabel's way; it will become a level plain before him! And when Zerubbabel sets the

> final stone of the Temple in place, the people will shout: "May God bless it! May God bless it!" (NLT).

God gives Zerubbabel courage to make a move in the present by giving him a glimpse into the future: "Zerubbabel will set the final stone in the Temple." For decades, no one could rebuild it. In fact, just about everyone was against it. But this prophecy assured Zerubbabel that though the local people may be against you, and enemies may be against you, and even the king might be against you, you *will* finish this work. Why? Because *God is for you.*

God gives us similar inspiration in Romans 8, in which Paul tells us how "for us" God really is:

> In the same way, the Spirit helps us in our weakness. We do not know what we ought to pray for, but the Spirit himself intercedes for us through wordless groans. And he who searches our hearts knows the mind of the Spirit, because the Spirit intercedes for God's people in accordance with the will of God (Romans 8:26–27).

The Spirit intercedes for us because *He is for us.* Through Him, we overcome our weakness.

Paul concludes his sit-down with us with these words, "What, then, shall we say in response to these things? If God is for us, who can be against us?" (Romans 8:31).

God told Zerubbabel, and He would say to every ReLeader who is willing to listen, that you can stay in the game and finish strong *if* you rely not on force or strength, but on the Spirit of God. He says He will level the unclimbable mountains that get in your way, making them into flat plains.

God is for you.

He is with you.

His Spirit will help you in your weakness.

And there is no mountain—there is no *anything*—that can stand in your way.

Grace, Grace

At the end of verse 7, it says, "When Zerubbabel sets the final stone of the Temple in place, the people will shout, 'May God bless it! May God bless it!'" That's not a phrase most people shout when a construction project is done.

A closer look at the Hebrew language in the text produces pure gold. "May God bless it" is translated from the Hebrew word *ḥēn*, which means, 'Grace, grace on it. Favor, charm, elegance.'

The grace of God makes the impossible *possible*. The grace of God lets you do the work of a ReLeader without losing your marriage, your kids, or your mental health.

> *The grace of God makes the impossible* possible.

If your ReLeader journey is causing you to produce bad fruit, then you're not doing it right. Zechariah was telling Zerubbabel what it was going to take for him to finish the work set before him. It was not by might, nor by power, but by grace, upon grace, upon grace.

If you're a ReLeader, this same grace is available to you if you will receive it.

- Do you need strength? God can provide it.
- Do you need wisdom and discernment? God can provide it.
- Do you need resources? God can provide that too.

You too will set the final stone in the rebuilding of your assignment, and it won't be because you were all that. It will be the result of you becoming the recipient of a supernatural grace that equipped you with everything you need to finish the task.

God will give you His grace because of four words:

God is for you.

Who Sent You?

A few years ago, some really dear friends invited Michele and me to dinner. They had done so much for us and had become very special to us. I told Michele before we left that we are going to buy their dinner tonight. "I don't care if it's $1,000—we're buying!" They invited us to a place in downtown Dallas called Nusr-et. If you've never heard of it, which we hadn't, it's the "Salt Bae" guy (just Google it). He's this strange chef who is famous for cocking his arm and hand in a weird way and sprinkling salt on steaks (who knew that's all it took to become famous). Little did we know that we had been invited to one of the most expensive restaurants on the planet. There is an entire section of the menu where the food comes wrapped in actual gold foil ... that you eat. (Again, Google it.) For a guy who grew up for a decent part of my life in a trailer home, this was jaw-droppingly dumb. Let's just say this dinner was going to cost *far* more than $1,000. I took one peek at the menu and looked over at Michele with eyes as big as saucers. When the check came, I will admit I did *not* jump to grab it too quickly. In that moment, I had never been more thankful for who had invited me to dinner. Because they sent the invitation, they intended to cover the tab.

When your heart is in the gutter and you're wondering if you want to get out of bed and go back in tomorrow, do you ever consider who invited you? It's easy to focus on the committee who hired you. You may wonder what they were smoking, or you might resent the lack of support you've received from them. But if that's who you're thinking of, then your mind is set on the wrong thing. Zechariah makes that clear.

A God-Assignment

Next, Zechariah tells Zerubbabel, "Zerubbabel is the one who laid the foundation of this Temple, and he will complete it. Then you will know that *the LORD of Heaven's Armies has sent me*" (Zechariah 4:9 NLT, italics added).

I want to encourage you never to forget who sent you on your mission, because it wasn't the hiring committee—it was the Lord of Heaven's Armies. That's big. If I'm sent on an assignment by a greater authority, then I carry with me a measure of the authority that comes from the one who sent me. I also have the favor and special assistance of the one who gave me my assignment.

From the inception of the assignment, when Haggai first called forth Zerubbabel and Jeshua in Haggai 2, God was making it known that when He invites you to dinner, He covers the tab. He assures us in Haggai 2:8, "'The silver is mine and the gold is mine,' declares the LORD Almighty."

Every ReLeader should find confidence to finish, knowing that it started and will finish, as a God-assignment.

Every ReLeader should find confidence to finish, knowing that it started and will finish, as a God-assignment.

THE WORK BEGINS

I love to see the work *completed.*

In fact, because there is so little closure in my leadership life, I've had to find things to do in my personal life that allow me to see a work from start to finish, all in one sitting.

My latest "hobby" is trimming trees in our yard, which has at least 50 trees in it. My wife laughs at me because I'm constantly looking out the window, picking out the limbs I'll remove next. Although it's grueling work, one of my favorite things to do on a day off is fire up my chainsaw and get to cutting. I will spend a few hours trimming, then I'll cut it all up, restock the firewood stack and burn the rest. Then when Michele and I go for a walk, I admire the work of my hands. I love that I get to see the job through to completion and be satisfied with my labor.

Leading rarely provides that sensation of closure because the work is never finished. Yes, occasionally a project is completed, but planning for the next one starts immediately. In ministry, it feels like every Sunday is the Super Bowl, and you have to do it 52 times a year.

ReLeading can be even more challenging. I've structured this book into nine step-by-step-by-step chapters, but the path to ReLeader success is never that simple. It's not always "up and to the right." It's more like "up ... and down ... and down and up and a weird, squiggly circle and up and up and down and wait, where did the line go?"

Adding to the discouragement is that sometimes ReLeaders spend nearly all their time building the foundation and then hand leadership over to someone else who will take it vertical.

The real test of our character as ReLeaders is whether we are willing to plant seeds that will grow into trees, even though we may never sit under the shade of or pick fruit from their branches.

That's often the ReLeader's fate, which is why Zechariah's next words are so meaningful for every ReLeader.

> Do not despise these small beginnings, for the LORD rejoices to see the work begin, to see the plumb line in Zerubbabel's hand (Zechariah 4:10 NLT).

Like me with the trees in my yard, our culture loves to see things *completed.* We celebrate pastors and leaders who have built great things—start to finish. That's why ReLeaders rarely speak at conferences or get invited to be on a podcast or get offered book deals. Our world rejoices to see the work *done.* But not God. That's why this prophetic word instructs us to not despise small beginnings. Zechariah tells us that "the LORD rejoices to see the work begin." God *rejoices* in

- the thing you're doing that is still just beginning,
- the thing you're doing that is "just foundation work," and
- the thing no one else can see, and even if they could, they wouldn't care.

Yes, God is jumping up and down rejoicing over that which may seem small and insignificant to you. So why would we despise what God is rejoicing over? Let's not call insignificant what God calls significant.

Let's not call insignificant what God calls significant.

God knows something we don't. God knows small beginnings lead to big finishes.

When Michele and I first got married, I became a professional home DIY (Do It Yourself) rebuilder. (I wonder if even in that God was birthing in me a desire to ReLead.) I learned how to lay tile and hardwood floors, texture walls, do trim work, and manage minor electrical and plumbing jobs. There wasn't a project I wouldn't tackle. DIYing created in me an appreciation for small details. Like, if you ever invite me to your house, I might admire the minutiae other people would never notice. *Wow, that was a really difficult tile cut that someone took the time to do. Look at the height of that ceiling, someone had to get up there and texture that wall!*

Find courage in knowing that God is for you, has assigned you, and is thrilled to see you begin this work.

I believe this is the heart of our heavenly Father. He is walking through your heart and your organization, admiring the small details of your leadership that are missed by the crowds. And God is rejoicing to see this small work begin. He rejoices because He knows the faithfulness it took and because He sees the big finish. So don't get distracted or discouraged. Find courage in knowing that God is for you, has assigned you, and is thrilled to see you begin this work.

NOW GET ON WITH IT

Zechariah spends all this time encouraging Zerubbabel, reminding him that God is with him and sent him. Zechariah was prophetically calling out Zerubbabel to finish the work. Then Zechariah issues a command: "This is what the LORD of Heaven's Armies says: Be strong and finish the task!" (Zechariah 8:9 NLT).

There comes a moment when there's been enough talking, and now it's time to be like Thor and pick up your hammer.

Just in case Zerubbabel didn't get the message, God repeats Himself. After saying "Be strong and finish the task!" the Lord says, "Be strong, and get on with rebuilding the Temple!" (v. 13 NLT).

It's a pretty clear message. God is saying, "Get on with it!"

Between those two commands, there's one more word of encouragement. In Chapter 4, I wrote how the prophet Haggai declared that the present house would be greater than the former one. Apparently, Zechariah now wants to provide a little extra detail to inspire the ReLeaders assigned to rebuild the Temple:

> But now I will not treat the remnant of my people as I treated them before, says the LORD of Heaven's Armies. For I am planting seeds of peace and prosperity among you. The grapevines will be heavy with fruit. The earth will produce its crops, and the heavens will release the dew. Once more I will cause the remnant in Judah and Israel to inherit these blessings. Among the other nations, Judah and Israel became symbols of a cursed nation. But no longer! Now I will rescue you and make you both a symbol and a source of blessing. So don't be afraid. *Be strong and get on with rebuilding the Temple*! (Zechariah 8:11–13 NLT, italics added).

Zerubbabel is given promises from God. *Fear not.* Your grapevines will be heavier. You will have bumper crops because the heavens will release the dew.

You are just beginning.
God sees the ending.
You worry that your work is insignificant.
But God rejoices to see the work begin.
So get on with it!

8

REbuild

GET ON WITH IT

> Among the other nations, Judah and Israel became symbols of a cursed nation. But no longer! Now I will rescue you and make you both a symbol and a source of blessing. So don't be afraid. Be strong, and get on with rebuilding the Temple! (Zechariah 8:13 NLT).

The women in my family love to put puzzles together. During many Christmas holidays they will spread a giant puzzle across the dining room table. Then my mom, sister, wife, daughter, and niece will randomly take turns putting it together.

If you've ever put a puzzle together (or even if you're a non-participating spectator like me), you will always find the box turned on its side close by. The box provides a picture of what the puzzle should look like when it's put together. The picture on the box serves as a template and guide. As you pick up a piece, you can analyze its color, design, and cut to determine where it fits in the grand scheme of the puzzle. Without the picture, it becomes nearly impossible to know where the pieces fit.

The picture is important because every puzzle is different. Some puzzles have 500 pieces while others have 5,000. Some are square, and some are rectangular. The puzzle may be a picture of a mountains, animals, or something else.

In this book I would really like to put a picture in front of you to help you put your puzzle together, but I can't. What is stopping me? *Every puzzle is different.* And as a ReLeader, you typically come on the scene long after the puzzle has been dismantled into a pile of pieces. Not only did you not get to put the original puzzle together, but there's no picture of what it used to look like or instructions on how to put it back together. Can you imagine trying to put together a 2,000-piece puzzle with no picture of what the finished product looked like?

We need a picture, but many times as ReLeaders we don't get one. Just ask Nehemiah.

Nehemiah and his fellow Israelites found themselves standing in so much rubble their strength was giving out. There were so many puzzle pieces to the wall, with no picture of how it looked before. They didn't even know where to begin.

If you're a ReLeader, you get that. How do you rebuild something you've never seen?

When Zerubbabel, Jeshua, and all who came with them returned to the scene of the previous Temple, all that remained were pieces of the puzzle. They did not receive detailed instructions for how to rebuild what was destroyed. They were only given a very vague guide in Ezra 6:3. King Cyrus declared that it would be "sixty cubits high and sixty cubits wide." That was it! Gee, thanks a lot for the specific blueprints.

Apparently, God didn't feel a need to give details about the design, but instead focused on their diligence to fulfill their calling as rebuilders.

Are you allowed to think something is funny that God says? I hope so, because I can't help but laugh when I read Zechariah 8:13. The first verse of the chapter says this was a word directly from the Lord to Zerubbabel and his team. In verse 13, after giving no specific instructions on how to do it, the Lord says, "So don't be afraid. Be strong, and get on with rebuilding the Temple!" (NLT) I didn't add that exclamation point, God did.

A few years ago, one of my pastor-mentors asked me, "Jon, how do you know what to do as a leader on a day-to-day basis? Could you write down a step-by-step process?" I thought about it and simply said, "I just do it, almost like it's instinctual." He nodded and said, "Part of it is gifting. Part of it is an anointing or empowerment from the Holy Spirit."

While that's true, it's hard to hear. We crave more specific direction. And yes, there are times when we receive strategy and wisdom from others. And yes, we can sharpen ourselves by reading books, listening to podcasts, or going back to school. But a big part of leading is: "Get on with it."

I know what you're thinking. Sure, I need to get on with it, but couldn't I just get some more direction first?

I get it. As I mentioned before, I love GPS. Honestly, I'm not sure how we used to survive without it. I appreciate the turn-by-turn directions and the elimination of surprises. I can look ahead and see every upcoming turn. I can zoom out and get reference and context surrounding the place I'm heading. GPS will even tell me when I am 800 feet, 500 feet, 300 feet, 100 feet, 50 feet, TURN NOW.

Isn't that awesome?

Sadly, in our tenures as ReLeaders, we rarely get to zoom out for context or look ahead at every turn we'll have to take.

It's not just you. Look throughout the Bible. How many people received detailed, turn-by-turn directions in Scripture?

- Noah was given the overall dimensions for the ark, but what about the small details? He had to step out and get on with it.
- God never gave Moses step-by-step instructions for how to lead the children of Israel to the Promised Land. Moses had to get on with it.
- Joshua wasn't given detailed instructions for how to possess the Promised Land. He had to get on with it.
- Elijah sat by a brook while ravens brought him bread and food as he awaited his next directive. He had to get on with it.
- The disciples were not given detailed instructions on how to plant the early church. They were given the Holy Spirit and told to get on with it.

We often don't receive specific directions; we get encouragement from God to get on with it.

We often don't receive specific directions; we get encouragement from God to get on with it.

Because we fear moving forward into the unknown, we sometimes look for excuses or even Bible verses that allow us to justify staying put instead of moving forward. One of the verses we often use is in Exodus 14. Moses is comforting the Israelites as their backs are against the Red Sea with the Egyptians pressing in on them. Moses says, "Don't be afraid. Just stand still and watch the LORD rescue you today. The Egyptians you see today will never be seen again. The LORD himself will fight for you. Just stay calm" (Exodus 14:13–14 NLT). We love this verse because we feel like it lets us off the hook. We don't have to do anything; God is going to move. And yes, move He does, but not without challenging us to move first.

As ReLeaders, we need to hear the next words from God's mouth to Moses. They're hilarious but also spine-tingling: "Then the LORD said to Moses, 'Why are you crying out to me? Tell the people to get moving!'" (Exodus 14:15 NLT). Again, with the exclamation point from God!

It's as if God was saying to them, *I'm going to move as soon as you get on with it. You can rest assured knowing that I am with you, and I will go before you, but you have to take a step.*

This initial step in the ReLeader process can be so daunting that it can keep you from moving. If you feel paralyzed by the fear of failure in your ReLeader journey, then I'd encourage you to go back and read Chapter 1 of this book. Remember that God called you.

You are anointed for such a time as this and for the organization God put you in to ReLead. And the Holy Spirit will do His greatest work through you *as you move.*

So get on with it! (I borrowed that exclamation point from God.)

GET ON WITH IT ... WITH A PROMISE

I want to break this passage in Zechariah 8 down a little more because locked inside is a promise to every ReLeader. Lean in because I don't want you to miss this. We've already discussed verse 13 (Get on with it!), and in verse 9, we find more of the same type of command:

> This is what the Lord of Heaven's Armies says: Be strong and finish the task! Ever since the laying of the foundation of the Temple of the Lord of Heaven's Armies, you have heard what the prophets have been saying about completing the building. (Zechariah 8:9 NLT).

More of the same. Be strong and finish. (Get on with it!) But now listen to what the Lord says in verses 10 and 11:

> Before the work on the Temple began, there were no jobs and no money to hire people or animals. No traveler was safe from the enemy, for there were enemies on all sides. I had turned everyone against each other. But now I will not treat the remnant of my people as I treated them before, says the Lord of Heaven's Armies (NLT).

Now think about this in the context of what you are trying to ReLead. Before you arrived at your organization, things were in chaos. It was in shambles, and leadership was required so rebuilding could happen. And here you are. You've answered the call, and God has anointed you for this critical moment in the life cycle of your organization or department.

So now let's catch this promise in verse 12:

> For I am planting seeds of peace and prosperity among you. The grapevines will be heavy with fruit. The earth will produce its crops, and the heavens will release the dew (NLT).

God was telling them, "As you step up, I will step in." He will plant seeds, and the grapevines will be heavy. The earth *will* produce its crop. This reminds me of Isaiah 55:

> "For My thoughts *are* not your thoughts,
> Nor *are* your ways My ways," says the LORD.
> "For *as* the heavens are higher than the earth,
> So are My ways higher than your ways,
> And My thoughts than your thoughts.
>
> For as the rain comes down, and the snow from heaven,
> And do not return there,
> But water the earth,
> And make it bring forth and bud,
> That it may give seed to the sower
> And bread to the eater,
> So shall My word be that goes forth from My mouth;
> It shall not return to Me void,
> But it shall accomplish what I please,
> And it shall prosper *in the thing* for which I sent it"
> (vv. 8–11 NKJV).

This is a powerful simile that gives us better understanding. Remember in third grade you learned about the hydrological cycle? No? It was when you learned about evaporation. You discovered how the rain comes down from the clouds and eventually evaporates back into the clouds for the next rain shower but not before it does its work on earth. Rain *produces*. It falls and does a work on the earth before returning to the clouds.

Many scientists believe that through the hydrological cycle, the water the dinosaurs drank is the same water we drink today.

It's the *same rain*.

God tell us in Isaiah 55 that the same is true with His Word. When God's Word goes forth, it produces. And it's the same Word.

- The same Word God spoke to Abraham, He speaks to you.
- The same Word God spoke to Moses, He speaks to you.
- The same Word God spoke to Paul, He speaks to you.

And God is speaking the same Word to you today that He spoke in Zechariah 8. The same Word, and it produces the same crop.

So let this Word go forth into your ReLeader assignment. You are called to this. Do not be paralyzed. Get on with it and watch the promise of God become your reality. You step up, and He'll step in.

Trust Him.

You don't have a GPS telling you what to do next, but trust His divine guidance. He has called you to this mission, and He will not let you down. Your perseverance will yield a harvest of blessings, and your dedication will bear witness to His faithfulness. Keep pushing forward, knowing that the grapevines will be heavy, and the fruits of your labor will be abundant.

Your perseverance will yield a harvest of blessings, and your dedication will bear witness to His faithfulness.

NOT EVERYONE WILL LOVE YOUR MOVES

The rebuild was underway! But it became clear that many were not impressed with how the Temple was looking.

> But many of the older priests and Levites and family heads, who had seen the former temple, wept aloud when they saw the foundation of this temple being laid, while many others shouted for joy (Ezra 3:12).

And let's be clear, they weren't wrong. To the naked eye, it *was* less impressive.

> Who of you is left who saw this house in its former glory? How does it look to you now? Does it not seem to you like nothing? (Haggai 2:3).

In the eyes of the "old-timers," it was incredibly disappointing. They saw the magnitude and greatness of Solomon's Temple. They saw hinges on the doors made of gold. There was no expense too great and no detail too small. They saw tens of thousands of laborers working around the clock. They saw kings from other countries providing materials. It was more than impressive; it was like nothing they had ever seen before. And rightly so—this was the Temple built for the God they served, the Creator of the universe and the God of Abraham, Isaac, and Jacob. To see it being rebuilt as anything less felt like an insult to their convictions and tradition.

Then God says something to realign their thinking and sets it all straight. "'The silver is mine and the gold is mine,' declares the LORD Almighty" (Haggai 2:8).

I used to think this was God telling them, *Don't worry about having the money to rebuild, because I will provide all you need.* That'll preach, and to be honest, that makes the ReLeader in us all feel a lot better. However, I think God is conveying something completely different in this moment. Please don't get me wrong—God *will* be your provider. God doesn't invite you to dinner without paying the tab. But we can't read a verse outside of its context. In Ezra 6, we see the decree from King Cyrus, allowing the Temple to be rebuilt. This is where we see the dimensions laid out *and* where we see how it will be paid for.

> The costs are to be paid by the royal treasury. Also, the gold and silver articles of the house of God, which Nebuchadnezzar took from the temple in Jerusalem and brought to Babylon, are to be returned to their places in the temple in Jerusalem; they are to be deposited in the house of God (Ezra 6:4–5).

God was *not* comforting them about the upcoming expenses of rebuilding the Temple. They were already paid for in full. I believe God was reframing their vision to see that what impresses man does not impress God. God was not impressed by all the gold and silver that adorned the first Temple. He owns it all anyway. What excites man does not move God. "His pleasure is not in the strength of the horse, nor his delight in the legs of the warrior; the LORD delights in those who fear him, who put their hope in his unfailing love" (Psalm 147:10–11). God is just not impressed by what impresses us. When Samuel was called to select the next king of Israel, God told him, "Do not consider his appearance or his height, for I have rejected him. The LORD does not look at the things people look at. People look at the outward appearance, but the LORD looks at the heart" (1 Samuel 16:7).

God is just not impressed by what impresses us.

The same is true with your organization, department, or whatever God has called you to ReLead or ReBuild. ReLeaders must look for a different measuring stick than what was used for the former house. Remember, the former house couldn't stand. As good as it might have been, there was something faulty about it that caused it to fall.

In the very next verse in Haggai 2, God provides a new measuring stick for success: "'The glory of this present house will be greater than the glory of the former house,' says the LORD Almighty" (v. 9). I wrote about this in Chapter 4, but again, from man's perspective, the present house may not appear to be as grand as the former house. However, God declares that the *glory* will be greater. The Hebrew word for glory is *kāḇôḏ*. It's the same word Moses cried out to God in Exodus 33, when he said, "Show me your glory." It can mean 'weight.' Moses was crying out, "God, let me see *all of you*."

This is our cry as ReLeaders too, isn't it? God, let me experience the weightiness and the magnitude of who You are. When the scales of my life are out of balance, and my circumstances have tipped the scales, weigh in on my situation. The glory this passage is speaking of is that weightiness.

EYE CATCHING

The first Temple might have been glorious in man's eyes, but the rebuilt Temple was glorious in God's eyes.

The question every ReLeader must ask themselves is, "Whose eye are you trying to catch? The eyes of man, or the eyes of God?"

I am a pastor, so let me talk pastoring for a minute. In God's eyes, the role of a pastor as a shepherd to their flock has never changed. But in man's eyes, the culture's definition of a successful pastor has changed.

Don't get me wrong—the *how* of pastoring can change, but the *what* never does. We might

- take a car to the hospital instead of a horse,
- keep notes in Evernote instead of a notepad, or
- preach from an iPad instead of paper notes.

But the *what* never changes. We spread hope, we love people, we preach the gospel, and we serve in the role of shepherds to the flocks we have been given. In essence, shepherds should smell like sheep.

But in the past few decades, there's been a shift in the mindset of what success looks like for pastors. In the late 1990s and early 2000s, we saw the megachurch burst on the scene. Hartford Institute for Religion Research defines a megachurch as any Protestant Christian church having 2,000 or more people in average weekend attendance.[1] I currently pastor what would be deemed a megachurch, so I'm certainly not bashing them. However, with the arrival of the megachurch model, something changed. Pastors became known. That's not necessarily a bad thing. Moses was known. Elijah was known. Peter was known. Paul was known. But something started to shift in the mindset of many pastors across

America. The measuring stick for success began to be tied more to the *size* of the church than the *significance* of the church. Success as a pastor became measured more by the number of campuses launched than the number of disciples launched. Success somehow became measured by the number of conferences at which you were invited to speak.

For centuries, pastors were shepherds. They were men and women who served a flock, without the temptation to compare flocks. Again, to put it in the words of Jack Hayford, "Pastors should be more focused on growing big people than big churches."

Yet somewhere along the way, without most even realizing it, the definition of a successful pastor changed, and shepherds became showmen. Young and upcoming pastors began to believe the lie that you're failing if your church isn't massive.

Why are we talking about this? Because as ReLeaders, we are not fixed on fame and fortune, but on faithfulness to our call. Remember the question every ReLeader must ask themselves? "Whose eye am I trying to catch? The eyes of man, or the eyes of God?"

God is far more moved by your surrender than your success.

What impresses men does not impress God. You are not a showman. You are a shepherd. Let me help redefine success for you. God is far more moved by your surrender than your success. We are called to sit in hospital rooms, not green rooms. You are *never* more of a pastor than when you sit on the side of a bed in a hospital room, holding hands with a family while their loved one slips into heaven. I have a green room too, but I fight to limit my time in it. Instead, I try spending more time out with the people God has called me to shepherd. Fight to keep the smell of sheep on you. ReLeaders are faithful men and women who do what they do because they are not trying to catch the eyes of men but the eyes of God.

LESS MAN, MORE SPIRIT

When I became the lead pastor of Victory Church, one of the core values we created was, *"We are not built on the talent of a few, but the sacrifice of the many."* We baked this into our culture because we wanted Victory Church to outlive me or any other leader. A leader who places themselves at the center must be revolved around. But Jesus is the only one who belongs at the center of your organization, and everything should revolve around Him. Small-minded leaders build their organizational branding around their big egos. (That's kind of harsh, but I'm going leave it in the book anyway.)

As you ReLead, REbuild, and REstart, be ever mindful of the need for more of His Spirit and less of yours.

I understand the need for a leader, and in some ways there must be one man or woman who steps up to be the primary leader. That's biblical. But we need to be cognizant of the tension that we do not belong at the center—Jesus does. If you're a big-headed leader, then you'll have a short-lived organization.

Back in Chapter 7, I told you that Zerubbabel quit the work of the Temple for 17 years. And the word of the Lord came to him, and one of the things God said was

> "Not by might nor by power, but by My Spirit,"
> Says the Lord of hosts (Zechariah 4:6 NKJV).

Two things are mentioned that you need less of—your might and your power. And there's one thing you need more of—"My Spirit." The best ReLeaders find ways to rebuild with less man, more Spirit.

I remember when I started my doctoral degree. I was looking over my courses and reviewing what it would take to complete the dissertation at the end of all of the course work. I felt completely overwhelmed, as if I were being asked to cross the Pacific Ocean with a (leaky) canoe and a (broken) paddle. Then my dissertation chairperson said something that's stuck with me all of these years. She simply said, "Stop looking at the elephant in front of you and just pick up your fork and take the first bite."

You may feel overwhelmed.

- If you're ReLeading a failed project, then this might take weeks.
- If you're ReLeading a department, then this might take months.
- If you're ReLeading an entire organization, then this might take years.

That's okay. Elephants are eaten one bite at a time. So fix what you didn't break. REbuild what you didn't tear down. REstart what you didn't stop.

Get on with it.

9

REinforce

HOW DID THIS HAPPEN?

It happened in April of 2014, but I remember it like it was yesterday. I was a campus pastor at the time and was driving to the church for an event when my phone rang. It was one of the executive pastors calling to tell me the news of our lead pastor's moral failure.

I was behind the steering wheel—I can vouch for that. But I'm not sure who drove the rest of the way. It must have been me, but I don't know how as my mind became completely void of thought.

In that one moment, with one phone call, everything changed.

Perhaps you've received such a phone call. One minute you were minding your own business; then, in a split second, your world stopped spinning, and your head started spinning. Your call might have been worse than mine. It may have been a doctor's report, or a highway patrol officer saying, "There's been an accident." And with that call, you felt as if your world crumbled.

For the Israelites living in Jerusalem, it wasn't a phone call. The world-stopping moment came when King Nebuchadnezzar showed up and destroyed what was most sacred to them. "He set fire to the temple of the LORD, the royal palace and all the houses of Jerusalem. Every important building he burned down" (2 Kings 25:9).

One day Jerusalem was business as usual. The next day there was total devastation.

Chances are, if you're a ReLeader, then you stepped into an organization that recently experienced a moment like this. You may not have been there when it happened, but today you find yourself standing in the rubble.

When you read a story like this in the Bible or experience it in real life, it makes you stop and wonder, "How did this happen?"

How did the Israelites allow their Temple—the most sacred thing to them—to be destroyed? Didn't they know that what they had built was sacred? Weren't they aware that an enemy would attack? Wasn't there something in place to ensure this would never happen? Wasn't there a wall to protect it? Wasn't there an army to protect the wall?

Those are great questions, and, yes, there *was* a wall. So how did the Babylonians get to the Temple? "The whole Babylonian army under the commander of the imperial guard broke down the walls around Jerusalem" (2 Kings 25:10).

What is the lesson here?

The enemy wants access to what's most sacred. He wants to attack the sacred things in your organization and to go after the sacred things in your life as well. Make no mistake, he will send an entire army to tear down that which is protecting whatever is most sacred.

The enemy wants access to what's most sacred.

THE SACRED AND THE SECULAR

What's sacred is, well, sacred. What's not sacred is, well, not. It can be easy to downplay what isn't revered.

If you lead a church, what is sacred would include God, worshipping God, and the gospel.

If you lead something other than a church, you might consider the *why* behind the *what* to be sacred. That includes those things that are essential to why you exist, your mission, and your vision for the future.

For the Israelites, the altar was the *why* behind everything they built. The altar was sacred, and people venerated it.

What about the walls around the city? They were practical. There was nothing holy about the walls.

That's true. And not completely true.

It's true if you ignore the significant connection between the walls and the altar. Yes, the altar was sacred, and yes, the walls were secular, which means "denoting attitudes, activities, or other things that have no religious or spiritual basis."

But both the sacred *and* the secular were needed to fulfill God's plan to restore the nation of Israel. Therefore, if the walls were incomplete, then the Temple was too. Without protective walls, the sacred was at risk.

In fact, in those ancient times, no city was complete without walls to protect it from bandits, wild animals, and invasions. In modern times, the more economically and culturally developed a city is, the more infrastructure you will find. For example, in large cities you will find a large and complex system of highways and roads.

In ancient times, the more economically and culturally developed the city, the greater the need for a wall. The Temple, with its lavish decor, would have been particularly at risk. If you don't prioritize the protective wall, then you've put everything in jeopardy. Once the walls are at risk, everything inside is at risk too.

The enemy is coming. He wants to destroy what's most sacred, but he'll often come first after those secular aspects of your organization that protect and prevent his access to the sacred.

What is that in your organization? Your financial procedures? Policies? Board governance? Accountability for leaders? Your staff culture?

What walls are still in disarray and need mending so you're not susceptible to the enemy's onslaught?

THE OTHER F-WORD

Perhaps I should congratulate you that you're still reading. I strung you along a little the first few chapters with a lot of, "You can't start yet! First you have to ..." and "You still can't start yet, because there's something else you have to do first ..." Then, finally, in the last chapter, I waved the green flag.

Any ReLeader might be tempted to take an apprehensive but excited sigh of relief, put down the book, and get to work.

But, like this book, you're not finished yet. Even if you've REbuilt, RElaunched, and REstarted, you're not finished yet.

This chapter, our last, is what separates the good ReLeaders from the best.

Green Flag at the Checkered Flag

Zerubbabel and Jeshua had engaged in a great rebuilding project with their eyes fixed on the finish line: the completion of the Temple.

> They finished building the temple according to the command of the God of Israel and the decrees of Cyrus, Darius and Artaxerxes, kings of Persia. The temple was completed on the third day of the month Adar, in the sixth year of the reign of King Darius (Ezra 6:14–15).

Can you imagine? All the work. All the time without the sacred. Now it's all over. Hammer in the last nail and let the celebration begin!

Except it wasn't all over.

Yes, the Temple was complete. And the Temple was most significant because it was sacred, so the Israelites felt like they were finished.

But they weren't, because they were missing a wall.

The Temple was completed in 516 BC, as recorded in Ezra 6:15. We're about to see that Nehemiah, who was appointed governor of Judea by the Persian king Artaxerxes I, returned to Jerusalem to rebuild the wall in the 20th year of the king's reign, which is believed to be about 445 BC (see Nehemiah 1:1–2). So for approximately 70 years, the Temple sat vulnerable to attack without a wall to protect it.

Think about that.

The Israelites were distraught when the Temple was destroyed. They went to great lengths to rebuild it, and then they *didn't* rebuild the walls, leaving the Temple vulnerable to another attack.

When Nehemiah heard that the walls of Jerusalem were still broken down more than a half-century after the completion of the rebuilding of the Temple, he "sat down and wept" (Nehemiah 1:4). Why was he crying? It was because he knew the job wasn't finished. Why would you work so hard to rebuild something and then leave it exposed so it could be destroyed again?

My guess is that it was because the wall was secular and, therefore, seemingly not significant.

Here's what I wonder: Is it possible you could successfully rebuild your organization, think you're finished, but ignore something that seems insignificant, which actually leaves you susceptible to another world-stopping moment when what is most sacred is destroyed again?

I know that after about four years of ReLeading Victory Church, we had done a significant amount of rebuilding:

- The staff was stronger than ever.
- My leadership team was in place and thriving.
- The attendance and finances had stabilized and were finally starting to gain momentum.
- More importantly, the Spirit of God was strong in our weekend gatherings, and we were seeing lives changed.

It was obvious that God was doing something beautiful and miraculous. But we were not finished.

If it was worth building, then it was worth protecting.

THE CULTURE WALL

God gave you a great gift that you probably never think about, unless maybe you start feeling a flu coming on.

I'm talking about your immune system, not Nyquil.

There are microbes that want to invade your body and make you ill, so God gave you an immune system as a line of defense.

Actually, that's not correct. Technically, you have *two* immune systems. You are born with your innate immune system. Your adaptive immune system develops over time after being exposed to various microbes. It literally keeps a record of every germ it defeats so it's able to recognize and destroy it if it ever shows its ugly face again.

Where in your body is your immune system? Everywhere. It's a complex system of cells and proteins produced in your bone marrow, tonsils, lymph nodes, spleen, and adenoids.

By the way, when you have a fever it's a sign that your immune system is working. And, speaking of it working, your immune system is not like a fine wine—it does not age well. As you get older, your immune system will shrink and work less effectively.

What does this have to do with anything (other than cold season)?

Well, just like your body has an immune system, a city in ancient times had a wall. The wall was designed to be a barrier to protect those inside and keep those who wish to do harm outside. It'd be great to have an army of soldiers guarding your city around the clock, but that isn't efficient or logistically possible. A wall can stand guard when humans' eyes are not available to keep watch.

And just like your body has an immune system, your organization needs something to protect what's inside your DNA, vision, and mission—and keep unwelcome things on the outside from getting in.

With the Israelites, it's obvious what the wall was because it was literally a wall. That's why Nehemiah cried when he discovered there wasn't one and committed himself to building one.

But what's the wall for us? If we don't know what it is, we probably won't be upset if it's missing and won't be dedicated to building it.

The most powerful, impenetrable wall of protection you will ever build around your organization is the culture you form within your organization.

Culture is not a wall that can be physically touched, but everyone can feel it. It's not a wall that can be eaten, but everyone can taste it. It's not a wall that can be scaled, but everyone can sit under its shade.

A healthy culture is the immune system to the living, breathing aspects of your organization. The immune system in your physical body is on a search and destroy mission. When you develop a culture in your staff and constituency base, they then become your immune system that seeks and destroys anything that is countercultural.

A healthy culture is the immune system to the living, breathing aspects of your organization.

Most organizations are built (or rebuilt) by great people with a great cause, but those organizations are vulnerable to attack because the focus has been solely on the cause and not the culture. The cause feels sacred, so it's prioritized. The culture doesn't, so it's not. But if you want to rebuild and protect the work you do so it's not later destroyed, you will be committed to building the right culture.

To do that, you may need to develop a new ReLeader's mindset.

THE RELEADER'S MINDSET

Two or three years along in my ReLeader journey at Victory Church, I began to sense a shift in my leadership mindset. At the time, I don't think I realized it was happening, but I see now that God was transforming my mind. He was giving me the mindset of a ReLeader.

I believe God planted four big leadership ideas in my heart during those years that formed me into the ReLeader I am and simultaneously created a culture to protect what God had rebuilt. I share these with you because I believe they will help you in your ReLeader journey.

1. Always Add "Interim" to Your Title

You are not the leader of your organization. You are the "interim leader." You are not the pastor; you are the interim pastor. You are not the president; you are the interim president. The title on your business card might read Vice President, Director, Lead Pastor, Chairman, Executive, or Associate. But the best ReLeaders always have the mindset that in front of the title on the card should be the word "interim." Why? Because whether you are in your role for one or 100 years, there will always be someone who sits in that seat after you.

Brady Boyd (one of the greatest ReLeaders I know) and I have talked many times about an interesting dichotomy we've seen in the mindset of Entrepreneurial Leaders versus ReLeaders. Most leaders who started their organizations struggle to see themselves as the interims. I get it. They were pregnant with an idea, carried it to full term, gave birth to it, bottle-fed it, changed its diapers, and watched it grow up. There were times when they paid the organization's payroll out of their own pocket. Time after time they sacrificed, bled, sweat, and clawed so their organization could reach the success it has today. In their mind, "It will always be my baby," and it can be very difficult for them to visualize anyone else at the helm of the ship. This can make things interesting when the time comes to name a successor. There might be delays in the timeline, micromanaging of anyone who takes the role, or forced succession to children who might not otherwise have qualified in a standard job search for the role.

For a ReLeader, the perspective is often far different. The ReLeader is well aware this was not their baby. They hold the organization with an open hand, knowing God has placed them there for a season to steward it back to health. They willingly and easily walk away when the Lord directs. ReLeaders know that there is always a *next*.

You may be wondering, *Sure, I'm with you. But why does seeing yourself as the interim help to protect your organization?*

When you lead with an interim mindset, it forces you to see beyond your short time there and focus on what will ensure longevity to your organization. You want to protect what you've built to ensure the organization outlives you.

You want to protect what you've built to ensure the organization outlives you.

The best ReLeaders are the ones who see their role as interim.

2. Build Guard Rails Instead of Hospitals

Have you heard the saying "It's better to build guard rails at the top of a mountain than a hospital at the bottom"? The church I was called to ReLead fell down a steep mountain and was hospitalized for about three years. As the interim pastor, how do I ensure we never fall down this mountain again?

Nehemiah knew that what had been rebuilt was sacred, and he wanted to build something secular to protect what was sacred.

One of the first things Nehemiah did was to inspect the walls of the city (see Nehemiah 2:11–16). After inspecting the walls, he identified the areas that were most vulnerable to attack (see Nehemiah 2:17–18). I don't think he had a camera and an iPad to take notes on, but you can believe he was taking notes and formulating a strategic plan to build something that would protect what was sacred.

At Victory Church, the fall of our leader involved infidelity. Recognizing that as a vulnerability, we wanted to build guardrails so we didn't end up in that hospital again. Here are just a few we put in place:

- I am not allowed to travel alone. When I go to speak at an event, the host is asked to pay for someone to accompany me. If they cannot, then Victory Church pays for it. This provides accountability and also protection from accusations.
- No one on staff is allowed to meet alone with the opposite sex. Any meeting between two members of the opposite sex is done out in the open. If that's not possible, if the meeting must be done in private or behind closed doors, it has to be in a room with windows or there needs to be a third person in the meeting. If a female and male are headed to the same location, they take separate cars.
- I have pastors and mentors to whom I am personally accountable.
- My wife has full access to my phone, email, and social media platforms.

We didn't build those guardrails because people on our staff are untrustworthy but because what we've rebuilt is too important to risk. Guardrails are not put on the sides of roads because someone is planning to run off the road but because they've seen the damage that can happen when someone does. Victory Church had tumbled down that mountain before, and we didn't want to see it happen again.

Your organization may need different guardrails. Perhaps you've had a software breach and need to put in firewalls to ensure that never happens again. Or maybe there was an indiscretion with your finances, and you need to add layers of accountability or remove or add someone as the signatory on bank accounts.

Don't wait any longer. Inspect the walls around what you've rebuilt. Where are you vulnerable? If it was worth rebuilding, it's worth protecting. Do your best as the ReLeader to ensure your organization never ends up in that hospital again.

3. What is Significant is Not Always Sexy

The Temple is done—finished. The ReBuild is complete. But there's one more thing to do. It's not sexy, but it's significant.

I wonder why it took nearly 70 years for someone to come behind Zerubbabel and Jeshua to rebuild the wall to protect what was sacred. Zerubbabel and Jeshua got to plan out, pick out, and lay out. They dreamed, designed, and directed. They thought about the crowd that would come and what they would experience. They were rebuilding a place where the very presence of God would come and people would experience hope, joy, community, and even the cleansing of sin.

What was left to do was not sexy.

Enter Nehemiah.

Nehemiah was a ReLeader who showed up and did what no one else was willing to do. He came to stand in the rubble and stack rocks.

- No one would ever glance at those rocks.
- No one would walk by the wall and marvel at the wall's brilliance.
- No one would experience any deep emotion or profound satisfaction from Nehemiah's work.

Building the wall, protecting what's sacred, isn't sexy, but it *is* significant.

ReLeaders develop a mindset that places significance over sexiness. ReLeaders develop the mindset of "Someone has to do it; someone has to be Nehemiah; it might as well be me." For the sacred to last, someone has to be intentional about building something to protect it. Without that protection, someone else might have to start all over again a few years from now. Without a Nehemiah, the enemy will come back and destroy the Temple all over again.

ReLeaders lean into things others lean away from. As we've discussed in previous chapters, ReLeaders are not looking for fame or fortune; they desire to be faithful. If you find yourself in a season that feels about as sexy as stacking rocks, please hear me saying that what you are doing *is* significant.

4. Be Careful Who You Let In

Parenting is hard work. (Can I get an Amen, parents?) When my kids were little, life was about keeping them *out* of stuff, such as hot stoves, sharp corners, long falls, quicksand, hot lava, tornadoes, and piranha-infested water. It was about keeping them out of harm's way until they could develop their balance and their understanding of what was safe and what was not. As I write this book, my kids are teenagers. And oh, how the strategy has changed. Michele and I have sharply turned our attention from keeping them *out* of harm's way, to trying to keep harm from coming *in*. It matters what they watch on their screens and what they hear in their headphones and, perhaps most importantly, with whom they spend their time.

When it comes to developing a healthy culture in your organization, I've found who you let in might be as important as who you keep out. A wall of protection is only as good as its gatekeepers. You can have impenetrable walls, but if the keeper of the gates lets in the wrong people, it won't matter how strong your walls are. (Ask Troy what they think about Trojan horses.)

Who you let into your organization matters. You could build one of the best organizations in the world, but the wrong person with the wrong motives in the wrong position could single-handedly bring it all down. Competency is important, but character and chemistry cannot be trained; competency can. It's better to have too few staff than to hire the wrong person because you feel desperate. Only let people in who have chemistry with you, who will live out your core values, and who have character above approach.

Who you let into your organization matters.

Your mindset in this season is mission critical to truly finishing the job. Your ReLeader journey is not complete until what you have REbuilt is REinforced and so protected from future attacks.

To summarize: Ask God to give you the right mindset, which I believe will include:

- **Add Interim to Your Title.** You're not building something for the now—you're building it for the next.
- **Build Guardrails Instead of Hospitals.** What can you put in place to keep your organization from ending up in the hospital again?
- **Not Sexy, But Significant.** Sometimes the most significant thing you can do for the organization is something everyone else is overlooking or no one else wants to do.
- **Be Careful Who You Let In.** Don't just build a great wall. Man the gates.

WHEN FINISHED IS FINISHED

The first words of this book said: "I would call you a leader, but you're more than that. That title, leader, is selling you short. It doesn't properly describe what you do. No offense to leaders, but you're something far greater."

Hopefully, you see that now. You grasp the significance and magnitude of what you're called to do.

You run toward the fire others run from. You face the aftermath, the remnants of shattered trust and disillusionment. You understand the road ahead is filled with challenges and obstacles, but you embrace them with determination.

You possess the gift of restoration—a remarkable ability to breathe life back into failed cultures. You bring healing, optimism, and a renewed sense of purpose to those who have been disheartened. You carefully analyze existing systems, policies, and practices, discerning which ones to preserve, modify, or discard.

Your strength lies not only in your adaptability but also in your empathy. You recognize that behind every staff member, every team, there are unique stories, experiences, and aspirations.

You have the audacity to envision a brighter future. You are not constrained by the limitations of traditional leadership roles. Instead, you redefine them, setting new standards of excellence and resilience. You forge a path for others to follow, leaving behind a legacy of transformation and progress.

You are a bridge-building, vision-shouting, team-uniting, heart-mending, culture-shaping, problem-solving, purpose-igniting catalyst for change in your organization.

Embrace the challenges, embrace the opportunities, and never underestimate the profound impact you can make.

You're not just a leader; you're a ReLeader.

References

Introduction

1. Yonat Shimron, "Study: More Churches Closing than Opening," Religion News Service, May 26, 2021, https://religionnews.com/2021/05/26/study-more-churches-closing-than-opening/.

2. Bob Smietana, "Thousands of Churches Close Every Year. What Will Happen to Their Buildings?," Religion News Service, March 15, 2022, https://religionnews.com/2022/03/15/thousands-of-churches-close-every-year-what-will-happen-to-their-buildings/.

1. REspond

1. Throughout the book I make reference to Greek and Hebrew terms that will help the reader gain a fuller sense of the biblical text. I have captured the meanings of these terms from www.blueletterbible.org.

2. Leif Heitland, "Healing the Orphaned Spirit," video, 22:43, April 4, 2012, https://www.youtube.com/watch?v=O41AbkNpB1o&ab_channel=PurePassionMedia.

3. REquired

1. Joshua Piven and David Borgenicht, "How to Survive If Your Parachute Fails to Open," in *The Worst-Case Scenario Survival Handbook: Expert Advice for Extreme Situations* (San Francisco: Chronicle Books, 2019), 137–39.

2. "38% of U.S. Pastors Have Thought About Quitting Full-Time Ministry in the Past Year," Barna, November 16, 2021, https://www.barna.com/research/pastors-well-being/.

3. Rick and Kay Warren, "Rick & Kay Warren Extended Interview," interview by Kim Lawton, PBS, September 1, 2006, https://www.pbs.org/wnet/religionandethics/2006/09/01/september-1-2006-rick-kay-warren-extended-interview/3647/.

4. Samuel R. Chand, *Leadership Pain: The Classroom for Growth* (Nashville, TN: Thomas Nelson, 2015), 35.

4. REassurance

1. Carey Nieuwhof, "6 Reasons You Feel Lonely in Leadership," CareyNieuwhof.com, May 4, 2023, https://careynieuwhof.com/6-reasons-you-feel-lonely-in-leadership/.

5. REfocus

1. Simon Sinek, *Start with Why: How Great Leaders Inspire Everyone to Take Action* (London: Penguin Books Ltd, 2011).
2. Patrick Lencioni, *Silos, Politics & Turf Wars: A Leadership Fable about Destroying the Barriers That Turn Colleagues into Competitors* (San Francisco, CA: Jossey-Bass, 2006).
3. Chip Heath and Dan Heath, *Made to Stick.: Why Some Ideas Survive and Others Die* (New York: Random House, 2010).

6. REestablish

1. Koride Mahesh, "Poor foundation caused collapse that left 11 dead," Times of India, update January 8, 2017, https://timesofindia.indiatimes.com/city/hyderabad/poor-foundation-caused-collapse-that-left-11-dead/articleshow/56396521.cms.
2. Stephen R. Covey, quoted in "Trust Is the Glue of Life: A Case Study in Building Trust," People and Performance Strategies, October 30, 2018, https://ppstrat.com/trust-is-the-glue-of-life-a-case-study-in-building-trust/.
3. Seth Godin, "The Most Important Question," Seth's Blog, December 17, 2020, https://seths.blog/2014/02/the-most-important-question.
4. James C. Collins, *Good to Great* (New York. Random House Business, 2001).

7. REmain

1. *The Steinsaltz Tanakh: Megillat Esther Mevohar* (Jerusalem: Koren Publishers, 2018).

8. REbuild

1. Hartford Institute for Religion Research, "Megachurch Definition," accessed October 2, 2023, http://hirr.hartsem.edu/megacshurch/definition.html.

About the Author

Dr. Jon Chasteen has a multifaceted background in ministry and academia. Since 2014, he has served as lead pastor of Victory Church, a growing multisite church with campuses in Oklahoma and Texas. He received a doctorate in university administration, which provided the foundation for his 12-year career in higher education. Within this period, he served as a university vice president of Southwestern Christian University and later as president of The King's University and Seminary from 2018 to 2023.

A common thread in Dr. Chasteen's leadership career has been a focus on ReLeading—taking the helm of established organizations to enact targeted improvements.

Dr. Chasteen is a dedicated husband to his wife, Michele, and father to their two children.

Subscribe to the ReLeader Substack and Podcast

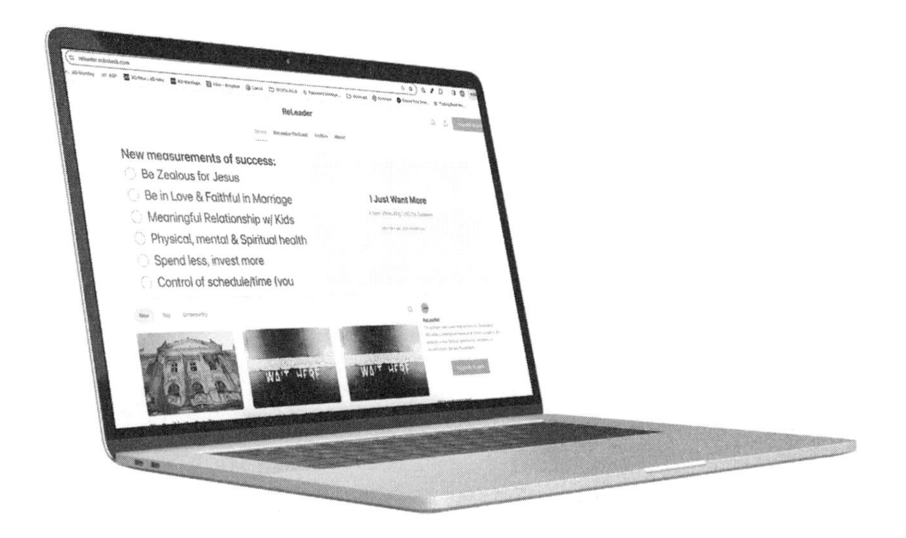

ReLeaders emerge to mend what others couldn't. We pick up the pieces, stabilize the environment, and set a new direction. We embody a new form of leadership centered on revitalization. We may not have launched the organization, but we have stepped in because it needed us. This inspired newsletter from Dr. Jon Chasteen provides resources and content for the individuals who find themselves in this critical position of ReLeadership.

Subscribe today at ReLeader.co!

LISTEN TO THE BUILT FOR WAR PODCAST

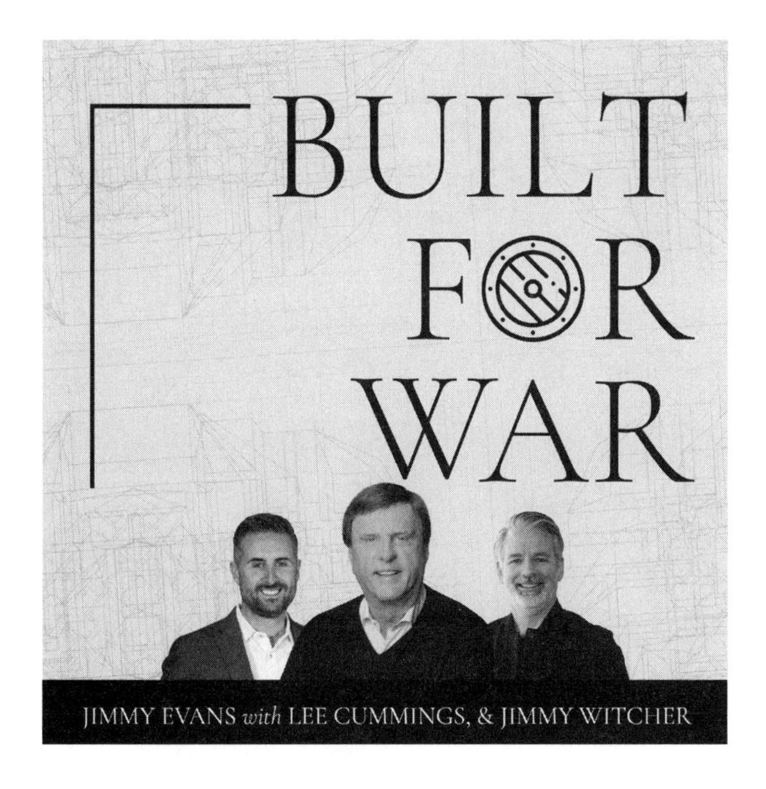

Built for War draws from Jimmy's decades of pastoral study, successes, failures, hard-won wisdom and front-line expertise to give insight for leaders both inside and outside the church. The podcast will focus on leadership topics within the church, the business world, nonprofit management, and beyond.

Find Built For War wherever you listen to podcasts!
New Episodes Monthly